THE CHAIRLEADER

THE CHAIRLEADER

LEAD WITHOUT LIMITS

CHRIS MALLEO
WITH **FRANKIE KINEAVY**

THE CHAIRLEADER
Lead Without Limits

Copyright © 2025 by Chris Malleo

Interior Layout and Design by Stephanie Anderson
Book Cover Design by Jess LaGreca
Editorial Team: Jim Sloan, Traci Matt, Becca Blackburn, Chloie Benton

ISBNs:
979-8-89165-283-5 *Paperback*
979-8-89165-282-8 *Hardback*
979-8-89165-284-2 *E-book*

Published by:
Gordon Publishing
gordonpublishing.com/

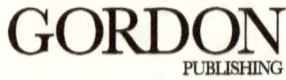

GORDON
PUBLISHING

This book is dedicated to Elizabeth Ann Malleo.
Your story, The Lost Backpack, *sparked a love of writing in me that I carry to this day. Through your words, you taught me the power of storytelling and how it can inspire, heal, and connect us. Though you're no longer here, I feel your presence in every word I write, and I hope this book makes you proud. Thank you for believing in me, for your boundless love, and for showing me how to live a life full of meaning. This is for you.*

CONTENTS

FOREWORD

WHEN I FIRST MET FRANKIE KINEAVY AT VILLANOVA, it was clear that he was someone special.

He didn't need a title or a position of authority to lead; his presence, his resilience, and his heart set a standard for everyone around him. Frankie was a student manager for our basketball program, but more importantly, he was a part of our family.

Through every early morning practice, every tough loss, every championship run, Frankie brought a spirit of perseverance and positivity that lifted the people around him. It wasn't about what he said, it was about how he lived. He faced challenges most of us will never fully understand, but he approached every day with an uncommon strength, an unshakable belief in others, and an incredible sense of humor.

When I heard about *The ChairLeader* and the journey Chris Malleo and Frankie shared, I wasn't surprised, I was inspired. What you're about to read isn't just a story about football or leadership. It's about what real leadership looks like: selfless, service-driven, courageous. It's about the quiet moments when strength is measured not in titles or trophies, but in character, resilience, and love.

Frankie has been teaching these lessons his entire life. And Chris, through his willingness to learn, lead, and grow, has brought those lessons to life in a way that will resonate far beyond the football field.

In a world that often rewards the loudest voice or the biggest platform, *The ChairLeader* reminds us that true leadership is found in how we serve, how we connect, and how we love. I'm honored to have been a small part of Frankie's journey, and I'm excited for you to experience the lessons he, Chris, and their team have to offer.

This isn't just a book you read.

It's a book you feel.

It's a book you live.

I hope it inspires you the way knowing Frankie has inspired me.

JAY WRIGHT
Head Coach, Villanova Basketball (2001–2022)
Naismith Hall of Fame Inductee and Two-Time
NCAA Champion

PREFACE

IT'S BEEN MANY YEARS SINCE I LAST DONNED A HEADSET AND PACED THE SIDELINE AS A HEAD FOOTBALL COACH, but my love for the game remains unchanged. Every August, as the fields are lined and the air fills with the whistle's shrill and the echoes of hard work, I'm transported back to the incredible experiences I had coaching, leading, and serving. I miss the game, the victories, and even the defeats.

But above all, I miss one of my best friends.

I can't walk past a football field without glancing toward the sideline, half expecting to see him rolling from drill to drill, his smile and laughter ringing with an energy so powerful it could stretch across a hundred yards and beyond.

Though we live in different parts of the country and no longer coach together, our bond remains as strong as ever. Coaching alongside *The ChairLeader* was one of the most beautiful experiences of my life. Through his example, I became a humbler man, a better leader, and, ultimately, a better human being.

They say you can't see the picture when you're in the frame, but looking back now, it's clear: We created something magical. We built a team and a culture so unified, so full of purpose, that even years later, those who were part of it still speak of it with awe.

That's why this story had to be told. For years, the seeds of this book have been buried in my heart—a desire to share something uplifting, something that might inspire someone else the way *The ChairLeader* inspired me.

I almost didn't write this book. If imposter syndrome were a person, it had me by the throat, dangling me off a cliff, whispering that I had no business sharing my story. "Who are you to think you have something the world needs to hear?" it asked. "What can you say that others more talented and qualified haven't already said?"

For a long time, those doubts held me back. Fear, insecurity, and the weight of self-doubt threatened to silence the story that had shaped my life. But two insights gave me the courage to move forward. First, I realized that the desire to write this book wasn't an accident. It was placed on my heart for a reason. Second, I learned that inspiration could come from unexpected places. You don't have to be a public figure, an influencer, or a world-renowned expert to impact lives. Sometimes, you find the most enduring lessons in the quiet corners of life, where ordinary people do extraordinary things.

I once heard someone say, "In life, you're most qualified to help the person you used to be." If you're reading this while struggling with your identity or questioning your purpose, I used to be you. If you're battling insecurity or fear, I used to be you. If you're navigating financial challenges, neglecting your health, or wrestling self-doubt, I used to be you.

Because I've been where you are, I believe I can help. Vulnerability isn't a weakness, it's a bridge. Our struggles connect us, reminding us that life isn't a silo of unbroken success. It's a paradox: pain and joy, struggle and triumph, heartbreak and fulfillment, all coexisting. What keeps me grounded in this beautiful chaos is my faith, my love for my family, and a nagging drive to leave the world a little better than I found it.

This book is about an extraordinary man who changed my life. It's also an invitation to embrace the lessons, struggles, and connections that make life meaningful. My hope is that when you turn the final page, your heart feels a little fuller, your soul a little lighter, and your perspective a little brighter.

Let me introduce you to *The ChairLeader*.

AN INTRODUCTION FROM FRANKIE KINEAVY

I AM LIVING A CHARMED LIFE. That might be hard for some readers to believe. But even though I was born with cerebral palsy, I feel like I got a pretty damn favorable draw.

I am the firstborn of Frank and Madeleine Kineavy, two of the most incredible people you'll ever meet. They are my rock, my foundation, and the catalyst for everything I have accomplished and will accomplish in life. Their story began one night at my father's restaurant, where they met, fell in love, and soon started their life together in Sea Girt, New Jersey.

To say Sea Girt at that time was a town out of a 1950s TV show would be an understatement. It was an idyllic small coastal community where everyone knew everyone, and kids rode their bikes until the streetlights came on. My dad ran one of the hottest restaurants on the shore, and my parents had just moved into a beautiful new home. In February 1991, life was pretty great for the Kineavys. Then I came along.

I won't bore you with the details, but let's just say my birth didn't go as planned. The umbilical cord wrapped around my neck, cutting off oxygen, and I entered the world blue as the ocean. Touch and go would've been optimistic. The doctors sent my dad home at three a.m., unsure if I'd survive the night. But as the story goes, by the time he came back, I'd pulled out my own breathing tube and was breathing on my own. For a guy who never wanted kids, that moment was the beginning of a life my dad could never have imagined.

The first decade of life with a kid with a disability can be the hardest on the parents, especially if there are siblings around. My mom's life became a whirlwind of therapy appointments, doctor visits, and navigating a world not built for kids like me. The social circles she once had disappeared, replaced by conversations with therapists and specialists.

Raising a child with disabilities isn't a solo effort; it's a team sport. My brother and sister were part of that team, sacrificing a lot without ever showing jealousy for the attention I received. They spent countless hours in waiting rooms, doing homework or coloring, while I went through therapy. Despite this, we grew close.

Looking back, I realize how easily things could have been different. But my parents were determined to give us as normal a childhood as possible. Because of their efforts, I not only grew up with siblings who are my strongest allies but also developed lifelong bonds with them. Today, they're both flourishing. My sister Annie is my go-to for career advice and Netflix recommendations, and my brother PJ, an Army Ranger, is my source for military jargon and obscure movie quotes.

I can't pinpoint my first memory, but it probably happened in a waiting room. My early life revolved around therapy, specialized schools, and interactions with other kids with disabilities. While I appreciated these bonds, I often felt disconnected. There was a gap between where I was and where I wanted to be.

That changed in 1996 when, after navigating small-town politics, my parents enrolled me in kindergarten at our local public school. It was a bold move. Being the first nonverbal wheelchair user at Sea

Girt Elementary wasn't without its challenges. On the first day, the teacher spent thirty minutes figuring out which table my wheelchair could fit under.

Despite these barriers, the school's small size—just 180 students—worked in my favor. At six years old, kids are more likely to accept differences, and my classmates quickly looked past my wheelchair.

My parents were relentless in ensuring I did everything my peers did. My dad, who had never touched a soccer ball in his life, spent Saturdays chasing down balls with me on the field. My mom, the oldest person ever to get stuck on the school slide, was equally dedicated. Their creativity and determination opened new possibilities.

One cold Saturday morning, after my dad nearly threw out his back helping me dribble a basketball for forty-five minutes, a coach for the grade above mine invited me to sit on the bench during their game. He handed me small responsibilities: deciding substitutions, suggesting plays, and offering advice. For the first time, I felt like I was part of the team, and I loved it. Week after week I returned, more excited to coach than to play. Sports became my bridge to belonging, and it opened doors to things I never could have imagined.

By high school, I was the student manager for the varsity basketball and baseball teams, gaining respect from peers who once saw me as "that kid in the wheelchair." My involvement shifted their perceptions.

The summer before my sophomore year, I attended a team camp at Villanova University run by Head Basketball Coach Jay Wright. Coach Wright impressed my dad not just with his mastery of basketball but with his ability to teach life skills, like making eye contact during a handshake. By the end of camp, he approached my dad and told him Villanova was known for supporting students with disabilities. Two years later, after a campus visit, Coach Wright called to offer me a position as basketball manager on his team.

Looking back, I wish I'd embraced that opportunity more fully. At the time, I thought college was my chance to step away from basketball and explore other aspects of myself. I missed the bigger picture: Working with Villanova basketball wasn't a limitation, it was a launchpad.

Still, I learned valuable lessons from Coach Wright, particularly about leadership. He had a gift for turning a group of individual superstars into one cohesive family. That principle remains a blueprint for how I approach leadership today.

In 2016, I found myself at a crossroads. I had a stable journalism job, but I wasn't happy. For the first time, I felt stagnant. I wanted more. I missed the sense of purpose I'd felt in coaching high school sports, so I decided to reconnect with that passion.

One day, I sent an email to several prep school football programs, introducing myself and detailing my experience. Only one coach responded: Chris Malleo from The Peddie School in Hightown, New Jersey. From our first conversation, I knew he'd play a significant role in my life.

Unlike most interviews, which focused on what I *couldn't* do, Chris wanted to know how he could leverage my strengths. We quickly realized my skills in research, analysis, and communication aligned perfectly with the unique demands of a boarding school football program. Over the next four years, we worked hand-in-hand to rebuild Peddie's roster and improve the program.

As Chris takes you through the lessons he learned from me, I want to share how my time with him altered my perspective. Working together taught me that success isn't about overcoming limitations, it's about redefining them and creating opportunities where others might see only barriers.

This book highlights many things I accomplished as part of the Peddie football coaching staff, but the truth is, none of them were done alone. What "we did" as a program was a collective effort, and at the center of it all was one of the most remarkable leaders I've ever had the privilege of working with: Chris Malleo. Chris didn't just create an environment where people could thrive, he led with such steady conviction, compassion, and boldness that he inspired all of us to reach beyond what we thought was possible.

The word "culture" gets thrown around a lot in both athletics and business, but the culture Chris built at Peddie was unlike anything I've ever experienced. For four years, I lived and breathed that culture, and it shaped not only our team but also me personally. Chris exuded leadership in everything he did. His style wasn't forced or performative, it was authentic, and it inspired everyone around him. He served his coaches, his players, and the school with a rare level of dedication and humility. He could have been leading a Fortune 500 company, yet he chose to dedicate himself to the fields of a quiet New Jersey prep school. At the time, I don't think any of us fully realized just how special it was to work under someone like him.

Most organizations reflect their leadership, and at Peddie, that leadership began with Chris. Chris didn't care how I got my work done; he cared about results. He didn't see my chair as a limitation; he saw it as irrelevant to my ability to contribute. What mattered to him was the quality of my work and how it impacted the team's success.

I'll never forget the first scouting report I submitted. It was decent, maybe even solid by most high school standards, but it wasn't good enough for Chris. He handed it back to me with clear, direct feedback: "When you redo this, don't think you're doing it for Chris Malleo or Peddie. Imagine you're sending it to Nick Saban and Alabama."

That moment changed my perspective. For years, people had set limits on what they thought I could achieve. Chris set no limits. Instead, he pushed me to imagine myself operating at the highest level.

Working for Chris was one of the toughest experiences of my life, but not because of the workload. It was tough, because for the first time I was being told, "You can do better." Chris wasn't interested in mediocrity. He didn't let me rest on what I'd already accomplished. Instead, he challenged me to see myself as someone who could achieve more, someone whose potential was far greater than even I realized.

His critiques weren't about tearing me down; they were about building me up. He saw a future where I could change lives not just in football, but beyond it. By helping others reach their full potential, he believed I could reach mine. That belief was both humbling and empowering, and it forced me to see my own potential more clearly.

I feel so fortunate to have shared those four years with Chris not just as a colleague, but as a friend. Our time together made me better in every way, and the chance to coauthor this book with him feels like the culmination of all we built together.

This book is more than a collection of lessons. It's a reflection of how lives can be impacted through leadership, service, and inspiration. These lessons are rooted in the experiences and people who have shaped me, and I hope that within these pages you'll find something that resonates deeply with your own journey.

This is the story of how two people—one navigating the world in a wheelchair, the other navigating the complexities of leadership—found a shared purpose. Together, we learned that when you have faith, vision, and courage, the possibilities are endless.

AN INTRODUCTION FROM CHRIS MALLEO

GROWING UP IN A SMALL COASTAL TOWN IN CENTRAL NEW JERSEY, I never imagined football would become such a defining part of my life. My father, an Italian immigrant and a standout high school running back, instilled in me a love for sports. He had carried the hopes of his family on his shoulders when he earned a college football scholarship. Despite his own success, he encouraged me to stick to soccer, baseball, and basketball—sports that felt safe and familiar. Football wasn't part of the plan.

But by eighth grade, a growth spurt changed everything. I outgrew the soccer field, both literally and figuratively. I made the decision to trade shin guards for shoulder pads and leap into the unknown. That first year of football was humbling. I was awkward and clumsy, a gangly kid trying to find his place in a sport that demanded strength and precision. But beneath the bruises and missteps, I found something I hadn't expected: belonging. By the end of that eighth-grade football season, I knew I'd discovered something I loved.

Football anchored me through high school as a place where I found purpose, focus, and identity. It opened doors I never imagined possible, including a scholarship to Northwestern University as a quarterback. From the outside, it looked like a dream: a full ride to a prestigious school, playing the game I loved.

But dreams have a way of changing.

I redshirted my freshman year, waiting, believing my chance would come. When I rose to number two on the depth chart the next season, it felt like everything was unfolding the way I had always pictured. I was one step away.

Then everything shifted. The coach who recruited me left, and a new staff came in with a new vision—one that didn't include me at quarterback. Little by little, the path I had dreamed of started to disappear.

I was moved first to linebacker, then to tight end. Not because I wanted it, but because it was the only way to stay on the field.

I tried to convince myself it didn't matter, that as long as I was on the field, I was living the dream. But deep down, I knew I really wanted to be the one leading the huddle, standing behind center, carrying the weight of the team on my shoulders. Instead, I found myself wrestling with a harder question: If the dream doesn't look the way you thought it would, is it still worth chasing?

My college career became a battle, not just on the field, but inside myself. Struggle. Disappointment. Redefining who I was, one hard moment at a time.

I'll never forget that frigid November afternoon at the University of Illinois, after the final game of my senior year. The sting of defeat clung to me, but it wasn't just the loss that hollowed me out. It was the end of everything I had worked for—the finality of a dream that, for so long, had defined who I was.

My suit was neatly pressed, my tie perfectly knotted, but it felt like a costume, a way to cover the heartbreak I carried deep inside. The frustration of the game, the ache of an unfinished story, and the fear of what came next all bore down on me at once.

When I stepped out of the locker room, I saw my father waiting for me. He had traveled all the way from New Jersey to be there.

His presence undid me.

I tried to hold it together, but the tears came anyway—tears that had nothing to do with just one game. They were years in the making. Dreams lost. Expectations unmet. And the unbearable pressure of wanting so badly to achieve the goals I had set out for myself.

This can't be it, I thought. I couldn't accept that everything I had worked for, everything I had dreamed of, was ending at just twenty-one years old.

Then, amid the cold and the heartbreak, I felt a hand on my shoulder. I turned to see Coach Ryan Kessenich, our coordinator of player personnel and development, standing there, always a calming presence. Throughout my time at Northwestern, there had always been quiet conversations—coaches, teammates, even opponents—wondering why I wasn't playing quarterback. I wondered, too.

He looked me in the eye and said, "You have the talent to play in the NFL."

It wasn't the first time I'd heard those words. Coaches had hinted at it before, here and there. But that day, after the final whistle of my college career, they didn't feel like a simple compliment. They felt like a lifeline. A reminder that maybe the story wasn't over yet.

From that moment, I became a lone traveler chasing an improbable dream: earning a shot as a professional quarterback. It didn't matter that I wasn't invited to the NFL Combine. I still believed there was a window of opportunity—however narrow—and I was determined to squeeze through it.

On the advice of former teammates and mentors, I packed up my things and moved to Arizona. The dry climate was part of it, but more importantly, Arizona had become a proving ground for long-shot athletes like me. Private coaches. Elite training facilities. And a growing network of undrafted hopefuls, all chasing the same impossible dream.

I didn't know a soul in Arizona, had no job lined up, and nowhere to stay.

A friend eventually connected me with Gary and Hope Stevenson. I thought I'd be crashing on a couch for a few weeks. Instead, they welcomed me into their home, giving me my own room, a seat at their dinner table, and something I didn't even realize I lacked: stability.

Hope's encouragement always seemed to come when I needed it most, quiet reminders of why I was there whenever doubt crept in. Gary checked in on my training each night, asking about my progress like a father would. They didn't just give me a place to stay, they gave me a reason to believe. In a season full of uncertainty, their faith in me helped me keep my own faith alive.

Every morning, I woke up with one thought: Keep going. Find a way to get noticed. Earn a shot—whether through a pro day, a mini-camp invite, or even a CFL or arena team tryout. Anything that could lead to a roster, a locker, and a jersey with my name on it. I knew the odds. I knew most players never made it past this stage. But for me, the dream was still alive, and that was enough.

That chapter of my life wasn't just about football, it was about discovering who I was beyond the game. Stripped of the structure and identity that football had always provided, I was forced to confront the bigger question: Who am I without it? In the quiet moments between training sessions, I wrestled with doubt, purpose, and the realization that my worth couldn't be tied solely to a roster spot. It was a time of uncertainty, but also of growth—a season where I learned resilience, adaptability, and the kind of grit that would shape the next phase of my life.

Years later, after I finished my playing career, I stood at a crossroads. Football had given me some of the greatest joys of my life but also some of my deepest struggles. It had shaped me, broken me, and rebuilt me in ways I couldn't fully understand at the time.

I didn't know it then, but everything I had been searching for—real leadership, real connection, real meaning—was about to show up in a way I never expected, because that path led me to Frankie.

You'll notice that Frankie doesn't say much in this book. But when he does, his words cut straight to the core. Communicating was difficult for him, yet it wasn't a limitation—it was a revelation. While most of us speak an average of six thousand words a day, Frankie communicated fewer than two hundred. That forced him to spend most of his time listening and processing, and in doing so, he developed a far more enlightened perspective than most of us could ever hope to achieve.

This book is about the nine lessons I learned from Frankie; lessons that reshaped not just the way I approached football but the way I now approach life. His unwavering strength and perspective taught me things I never expected to learn about leadership, about trust, and about the kind of person I wanted to be. My hope is that these lessons will resonate with you as deeply as they have with me. If you apply them, I believe they can transform your life, just as they transformed mine.

This is more than a story about football. It's a story about resilience, selflessness, and the power of leadership rooted in love and understanding. It's about Frankie, about the team we built together, and about the life-changing lessons I'll always carry with me.

THE BEGINNING

IN THE WINTER OF 2015, I had just completed my first season as head football coach at The Peddie School, and I felt like a fraud.

I'd landed the job I thought I wanted. The title sounded impressive. But I didn't feel like a leader. Not yet. I was still just a guy trying to outrun his doubts. I was young and insecure. Still trying to figure out who I was. I didn't step into that role full of confidence, I stepped in full of questions. About the team. About the program. But mostly about myself.

What made it all feel even more complicated was where I had come from.

Just a year earlier, I'd been coaching at The Lawrenceville School—one of Peddie's oldest rivals. Lawrenceville had more history, more prestige, more stability. It was a program with resources and tradition, and we regularly beat Peddie. From the outside, it looked like I was walking away from the better situation.

But I wasn't chasing comfort. I was chasing the challenge. There was something about Peddie that drew me in. Something about the idea of taking over a program that wasn't expected to win. I relished the opportunity to build a team from the ground up, to reshape a culture, to lead as an underdog. That's what excited me. That's what made it feel real.

I'd played high school football at The Hun School, another prep powerhouse just up the road. I knew this world. I'd lived it. But back then, I was the kid chasing a scholarship. Now, I was stepping back into it as a man, this time with the responsibility to build something for others.

Football and I had a complicated history. It had given me so much, but it had also broken me. My body. My confidence. My dreams. I was talented, but my playing career hadn't gone the way I'd imagined. Coaching became a kind of therapy, a conduit to stay connected to the game and to people in a deeper, more meaningful way. I didn't know what I wanted to do with my life. But for those two or three hours a day on the football field, I felt found. Anchored. Like I mattered.

And then came Peddie.

Peddie is a small, yet storied, private institution nestled in a quiet town in central New Jersey. Founded in 1864, it boasts a rich tradition of academic excellence and is part of an elite consortium of boarding schools that defines the educational landscape of the northeastern United States.

The campus, spanning 280 picturesque acres, is a harmonious blend of history and prestige. The stately brick facades of the academic buildings and dormitories evoke a timeless charm, while the school crest and the iconic bell hanging in Ayer Memorial Chapel serve as enduring symbols of tradition and pride. The grounds, thoughtfully designed, create an idyllic setting that encourages the free movement of students and faculty alike, fostering a vibrant and familial environment.

It's difficult to properly articulate the atmosphere, but it radiates a profound sense of belonging and purpose, a place where the past and present seamlessly converged to inspire those fortunate enough to be part of its community. Walking around campus, you can feel the weight of history, as if it were gently tapping you on the shoulder, urging you to build upon the foundation so carefully laid by generations before.

At the heart of the campus stands Schuman Football Field, a sanctuary of tradition and aspiration. Its 120 yards of pristine Kentucky bluegrass gleam in the sunlight, a testament to the care and pride that define every corner of Peddie. But to me it was more than just a football field; it was a magnificent sight, a stage where dreams and determination collided.

Peddie was hardly known for the success of its football program. The head coach before me was a wonderful and talented man who poured his heart into elevating the team. Despite his best efforts, he was limited in what he could achieve. The student body consisted of 380 students representing twenty-two states and twenty countries, a diverse but modest population.

When you combine the small headcount with Peddie's strict admissions standards and the need to attract talent in the arts and other athletic programs, it became a significant challenge to consistently field a football team. Building a competitive program in such an environment required more than determination; it demanded creative solutions and a deep commitment to the school's mission and community.

Shortly before I was named head coach, the program had been mired in controversy. The team was forced to forfeit games due to low participation, a decision that left many parents disenchanted. Their frustrations spilled into the local newspaper, where they voiced their displeasure with the program's direction. It was far from an ideal situation to step into.

To complicate matters even further, not long after I accepted the position, the athletic director who had hired me left for another role.

By the end of our first season, I felt the enormity of the role I had accepted—a pressure that, in hindsight, I admit was largely self-inflicted. I was burned out. In addition to serving as head football coach, I worked in the admissions office and oversaw a senior boys' dorm as a dorm supervisor. While I thoroughly enjoyed each role, they stretched me thin, leaving little energy by day's end.

My focus on winning had consumed me, and in the process, I lost sight of who I was. Driven by ego and a desperate need to prove my worth as a head coach, I took on too much, rarely delegating responsibilities. I tried to control every aspect of the program. I coached every position, ran every drill, sat in on every meeting, and obsessed over every detail. I was constantly trying to do it all, because deep down, I thought that's what a "real" leader did. But the more I tightened my grip, the more I lost touch with what truly mattered: building trust, empowering my staff, and forming authentic relationships with my players and the broader community.

Although we finished the season with a winning record and the program was trending upward in the win-loss column, I was floundering. On the surface, things looked good. But beneath it, I was running on empty. I wasn't sleeping well. I'd come home exhausted but unable to shut my mind off. The things that used to bring me joy—time with family, working out, even being on the field—felt like obligations instead of outlets. I knew something had to change. During the offseason, one of my main priorities became bringing new talent to our coaching staff; people I could trust, lean on, and build with.

At this point, a new athletic director had been hired, a decision that proved to be a turning point. He quickly became a trusted sounding board and an exceptional leader in his own right. He believed in me and in the vision I was working to create. With his support, the administration approved a budget that allowed me to hire three new coaches, an exciting and rare opportunity.

When I took the job, I had inherited most of the previous staff. They were fantastic men who excelled at building relationships with our players, but I needed a few coaches who not only shared my vision but also saw and approached the game the way I did. This was a pivotal step in reshaping the program and aligning it with the culture and strategy I hoped to instill.

I posted a job opening, and the flood of responses was overwhelming. The candidates included former college stars and current and former college coaches. I was stunned by the quality of the applicants, each bringing unique and relevant football experience to the table. Sifting through the mountain of resumes quickly became a job in itself, but with each new application, my confidence grew.

The caliber of coaching talent available reinforced my belief that with the right coaches and our returning athletes, we could compete for a championship.

Two weeks after posting the job, I had a comprehensive list of candidates and planned to start interviewing the following Monday. As I started to delete the posting, a late email popped up on my screen.

The subject line read: Coaching Interest.

Too late, I thought, my finger hovering over the delete button. But something made me pause. On a whim, I clicked on it.

The email was from a young man named Francis Kineavy. In it, he laid out his case for joining our staff and attached a brief resume. He was young and had no real football coaching experience. His coaching background was mostly limited to high school basketball. But what caught my attention was his time at Villanova University, where he had served as a student assistant for the men's basketball program under the legendary Coach Jay Wright.

Impressive, I thought. Not for football, but certainly for his exposure to one of the greatest minds in sports. Still, his resume didn't scream "future football coach." What stood out was the sincere, authentic, and refreshingly humble tone of his email. Many candidates had written with a sense of entitlement, but this message conveyed a genuine desire to contribute and learn.

I offered him my last interview slot. My expectations were low, but perhaps I could glean some insights about Coach Wright and see if any of his philosophies could be applied to our program.

The following Monday, candidates paraded through my office all day, each more impressive than the last. I met several talented, qualified coaches, and several interviews ran longer than scheduled, putting me behind and leaving me bleary-eyed and drained.

By the time the final candidate was set to arrive, everyone in the athletic department had gone home and it was dark outside. I was starving. Why had I scheduled this last candidate?

My final candidate was Francis Kineavy, the guy whose email I'd almost ignored. He was a few minutes late. As I walked to the clear glass doors of the athletic office, I spotted a tall man casually dressed, his weathered face framed by wispy white hair poking through a sun-worn visor. He looked more like someone on his way to a Jimmy Buffet concert than someone preparing for a coaching interview. My confusion must have been evident, because as I opened the door the man immediately extended his hand with enthusiasm and said, "Hi, I'm Tim. I'm Frankie's driver."

Frankie's driver? The words seemed to echo, suspended in the silence, as I worked to comprehend what they truly meant. Before I could respond, a young man in a motorized wheelchair emerged awkwardly from behind Tim, slowly making his way toward me.

Tim, with impeccable timing and a warm smile, introduced us. "Coach Malleo, this is Frankie Kineavy."

Frankie extended a partially limp hand, his head cocked to one side, drool trickling from his chin. His kind eyes and gentle smile softened the moment, but I was frozen in time, completely caught off guard. Frankie was disabled, and here he was, offering me his hand while I struggled to comprehend why someone in a wheelchair who couldn't speak would be interviewing for a football coaching position.

I'd been around people with disabilities before and had even volunteered with the Special Olympics, but this felt different—raw, real, and entirely unfiltered. I wasn't prepared for it.

Awkwardly, I shook his hand, mumbling, "Nice to meet you," while still trying to process the situation. Frankie's wheelchair was large and bulky, with a plastic board affixed to his lap. The board had a clear plastic cover revealing the letters of the alphabet. He gestured for me to come closer, signaling that he wanted me to read his board.

Leaning in, I watched as Frankie, with painstaking effort, used a clenched, curled hand to point to each letter, slowly spelling out his words.

N-I-C-E T-O M-E-E-T Y-O-U T-O-O.

It was deliberate, challenging, and humbling to witness. As the words formed, I felt a wave of emotions—discomfort, curiosity, and an unexpected sense of admiration—rise within me.

We settled around the large oak table in the staff room where many of our coaching meetings were held. Frankie took his place at the head of the table, not out of formality, but because his bulky wheelchair made it too cumbersome to position anywhere else. The room, usually filled with the lively banter of coaches, felt unusually still as we prepared for what would undoubtedly be a unique interview.

Frankie was born with cerebral palsy. His motor functions were severely limited, and he needed round-the-clock assistance for nearly everything most of us take for granted—eating, drinking, even moving. The only way he could communicate was by slowly spelling out each word, letter by letter, on the alphabet board. What I expected to be a half-hour interview stretched into two.

I'd ask a question. Frankie would glance at the board, then lift his hand with effort and guide it, often with the edge of his fist or knuckle, toward a letter. One. Letter. At. A. Time.

Tim sat beside him, tracking closely. "F-O-O-," he murmured, glancing at Frankie, waiting. "T- B-A-L-L."

"Football," Tim confirmed, smiling. "He wants to talk about football."

We all smiled. I asked another question. Frankie went back to work.

Sometimes, Tim misread a letter or skipped a beat, and Frankie would let out a small grunt; not quite frustration, but insistence. A firm shake of the head. A sharp blink. He was locked in. Precise. You could feel it. This wasn't just communication. This was expression through sheer willpower. And we had to keep up.

Letter by letter, response by response, Frankie's world came into focus. He loved sports, especially football. He told me about his high school days, how he'd fought to take honors classes and upon graduation was admitted to Villanova University, where he played a key role in building a program that would help future students with disabilities navigate and thrive on campus.

By the end of the conversation, I'd stopped thinking about how long it was taking. I stopped noticing the alphabet board. Frankie's presence, his intellect, his dry sense of humor filled the room. He didn't just earn

my admiration. He made me forget why it was
ever in question.

But as meaningful as our time together had
been, I couldn't shake the realization that I
wasn't going to hire him.

Nothing Frankie offered translated directly
to the role. I had a responsibility to my players,
my staff, and the school. I was trying to build a
powerhouse football program, and my schedule
was already stretched thin. The idea of adding someone to the staff
who needed that much time just to communicate felt unrealistic. I
thought he would slow us down.

> He didn't just earn my admiration. He made me forget why it was ever in question.

He didn't know our scheme. He wasn't well-versed in strategy.
He couldn't run a position group. Who would manage him? How
would he get across campus? Travel to games? How would the staff
respond? The players?

I had already identified three strong candidates for the open posi-
tions. The athletic director had made it clear: There was only room for
three hires. Saying yes to Frankie would mean turning away someone
who could help us win games, and at that point in my life, winning
still felt like everything.

When the interview ended, I thanked Frankie and Tim for their
time and shook Frankie's hand again. It was awkward; I could feel
it in the silence that lingered a second too long. I told them I'd be in
touch, though I had no idea what I would say when that time came.

I offered to walk them out, and we left my office in silence. Frankie's
wheelchair moved slowly past the encased Heisman Trophy—a trib-
ute to Peddie alumnus Larry Kelley, one of the earliest recipients
of college football's most prestigious award. He continued past the
captain's boards—long wooden panels painted deep blue, with each

team's leaders' names hand-lettered in gold by the same family for generations. Then came the retired jerseys, framed and still, hanging like quiet sentinels of the school's storied legacy.

When he reached the large school crest emblazoned on the floor at the center of the room, his chair stopped. He turned his wheelchair to face me, his kind eyes meeting mine as Tim read aloud the words Frankie had painstakingly typed: "I know I can help you."

With that, they were gone.

A part of me was relieved it was over. But another part of me carried something heavier as I began to walk away. I returned to my office, shut the door, and pulled down the shade. I needed a moment to process what had just happened.

In the stillness, I was overcome. Tears streamed down my face, tears of gratitude for what I had, and tears of sadness for a man who had faced unimaginable challenges yet radiated nothing but courage and hope.

For a moment, I wanted to chase them down in the parking lot. I wanted to tell Frankie that I believed in him. That he was amazing. That life wasn't fair. That he deserved more than what the world had handed him.

But I didn't move.

I sat there, wrestling with the weight of it all.

As the tears subsided, my mind began to clear. And that's when it hit me: It wasn't that I couldn't hire him, it was that I wouldn't. But why?

I had all the reasons lined up—the communication hurdles, the logistics, the demands of running a competitive program. But then a new question emerged. A quieter one. One I hadn't let myself ask until that moment: What about the reasons it could work?

I closed my eyes, and images started to form. I pictured a group of sweaty, grass-stained players gathered around Frankie's chair, listening closely as he spelled out sharp, concise coaching points. I saw students holding doors open for him as he made his way across campus, not out of pity, but out of genuine respect. I imagined him at our staff meetings focused and prepared, his insights cutting through the noise. I pictured him and me sitting in this very office on a quiet Sunday morning, breaking down film together, his observations challenging my perspective and making us all better.

There was a peacefulness to it all. A stillness. Like the world had finally slowed down just enough for people to actually see one another. To hear each other. To connect.

Maybe that's what our team needed. Not just another coach, but someone who would stretch us. Ground us. Remind us what really matters.

Our team needed someone like Frankie. Our school and our community needed someone like him. And maybe, more than anyone else, I needed him.

I opened my laptop and began drafting an email to the athletic director, listing the three people I wanted to join the coaching staff for the upcoming season. My fingers hovered over the keyboard for a moment before I began typing, slowly and deliberately, as if each keystroke was a way of connecting to him:

F-R-A-N-C-I-S K-I-N-E-A-V-Y.

I hit send.

And just like that, *The ChairLeader* was born.

Frankie wasn't just a coach in a wheelchair. He was a force. A leader who didn't need to stand to take a stand. Who didn't need to run to move people. Who didn't need a whistle to command a room. We didn't call him *The ChairLeader* because of his chair, we called him that because of the way he led from it. With courage. With wisdom. With heart. It wasn't just a nickname. It became a philosophy. And it changed everything.

Over the next four years, what we accomplished as a football program was a direct reflection of Frankie's impact. But more than the wins, the championships, or the culture we built, what mattered most was the change in me. Who I was as a man, husband, and father was fundamentally reconstructed because of him.

You Are Significant

Success in life isn't about yourself, significance is about others. I want you to not only be successful in this life, but I want you to have significance... and that starts with impacting and loving the people around you.

—TIM TEBOW

I THOUGHT I UNDERSTOOD VALUE.

I thought it lived in scoreboards, accolades, scholarships, and stats. I thought it was something you earned—something you proved.

Then came Frankie.

He didn't just change my team. He changed me.

Not in a metaphorical, abstract way, but in a way that shook the foundation of how I saw people, including myself. He shattered the scoreboard I'd spent most of my life carrying in my head. And what he left in its place was a question I couldn't ignore: What makes someone truly significant?

Frankie helped me ask it. But the journey toward the answer? That started long before him.

It started in the summer of 2003 when I first stepped onto the campus of Northwestern University with big dreams, a bigger ego, and no idea how badly I needed to be broken.

I was a kid with promise. Standing six feet, three inches tall, weighing 225 pounds, I'd just been named the Prep Offensive Player of the Year in New Jersey after throwing for over three thousand yards, rushing for another eight hundred, and accounting for thirty touchdowns. Programs like Boston College, Notre Dame, and Iowa recruited me as an athlete, but Northwestern saw something different. They saw me as the quarterback of the future. I was raw, but talented. And I was ready to prove I belonged.

As a freshman, I redshirted and sat fifth on the depth chart while the team fought its way to a 6-6 record. It was humbling, but I kept my head down and went to work. By the following spring, I came ready to compete. I'd made real strides. I was still raw, but my size, athleticism, and arm strength gave me a shot.

By the end of spring ball, I was second on the depth chart just behind a junior entering his third season as the starter. My confidence soared after a standout spring game where I led the team in passing yards and threw two touchdowns against the first-team defense.

The future felt bright. I could see it. I was ready.

But that moment—the one I had worked so hard for—never came.

The offensive coordinator who had recruited me left for another job, and his replacement brought a different energy, one that lacked professionalism, consistency, and character. He had his own agenda, favored the players he'd recruited, and slowly made my life on the team unbearable. The joy I'd always found in football faded and was replaced by frustration, disillusionment, and emptiness.

Determined to find a fresh start, I explored transferring. But between complications with transfer credits and the unpredictable nature of college recruiting, I couldn't secure a new home. What once felt like a promising journey now felt stalled. The passion was gone. The future was foggy. And for the first time in my life, football felt more like a burden than a gift.

I stood on the sidelines of Big Ten games surrounded by eighty-thousand screaming fans, and I had never felt lonelier.

The accolades were gone. The spotlight had moved on. And with it, the identity I'd built began to crack.

That's when I realized something I never wanted to admit: The significance others saw in me was never really about me. It was about what I could do. And when the game stopped going my way, I stopped feeling like I mattered. Football had become my identity, and without it, I didn't know who I was.

Looking back, I know those coaches were wrong in how they evaluated me. I never lost faith in my ability. I'd spend the next three years grinding at linebacker and tight end, and the adversity forced me to confront the fragile foundation I had built my identity on, one made of completion percentages, forty-yard dash times, depth charts, and highlight reels. I had spent years believing my value was tied to measurable outcomes; to the way coaches ranked me, the way fans cheered, or the stats printed next to my name. When those things were stripped away, I was left asking a terrifying question: Who am I if I'm not producing?

It was a painful reckoning. But slowly, I began to see that my worth had to come from something deeper. Something unshakable. Not the scoreboard, but the strength of my relationships. Not my spot on the depth chart, but the quiet, consistent work I put in each day. Not how others saw me but how I chose to show up for the people around me.

As I processed that hard truth, I made a promise to myself: If I ever became a coach, I wouldn't let my players believe their value was tied to stats, wins, or athletic ability. I would help them see they were so much more than the number on their jersey or their performance on the field.

I wanted them to know what I had to learn the hard way: that their significance isn't tied to what they do, it's tied to who they are. And more than that, I wanted to help them uncover the unique impact they could make in the world. Not just as athletes, but as men. As teammates. As people who matter.

When I hired Frankie, I hoped his presence would do more than strengthen our football program. I believed he could inspire our players to grow into the most significant versions of themselves. He stirred something in me, and I was confident he'd do the same for them.

What I didn't realize was how much more I had to learn. Not just about coaching. About leadership. About humility. About presence.

Frankie didn't roll into our program to prove anything, he simply showed up as he was. And that, somehow, changed everything.

One of my earliest lessons came just after Frankie joined the staff. We were in a roster meeting, a critical but taxing exercise where we review each player's strengths, weaknesses, and potential. The goal was simple: identify how we could help each young man grow during the offseason and, in turn, strengthen the program.

From day one the staff welcomed Frankie, and he adjusted quickly, but he was still finding his place and his voice. While the general tone of his hiring was warm and supportive, it wasn't without its setbacks. Meetings stretched longer as everyone adjusted their routines and communication styles. Early on, side-eyes and raised eyebrows often flickered around the room as we slowed to read Frankie's board. For someone like me—obsessed with time management and organization—this hire was putting all of it to the test.

As we worked our way down the list, we eventually reached the fringe of the roster, a sophomore JV quarterback named Aidan McHugh. Everyone recognized Aidan for his heart, drive, and attitude, but his physical skills hadn't caught up to his potential.

I was more familiar with Aidan than most of our staff was. A year earlier, I had been in the center of a pivotal conversation with our admissions team, discussing potential candidates for the prestigious Armellino Scholarship—a full-tuition scholarship that covered a student's entire tenure at Peddie.

The scholarship was named after Michael Armellino, a Peddie and University of Pennsylvania graduate who had earned his fortune as one of the greatest stock pickers in history during his time at Goldman Sachs. Michael was a generous man with a deep love for Peddie and its students. Selecting a recipient for this scholarship wasn't just a process; it was a profound responsibility, one that none of us took lightly.

While I had a wonderful professional and personal relationship with my colleagues, admissions discussions could turn tense when you were advocating for someone you truly believed in. That morning, the room was filled with focus.

I sat there quietly, listening as our team discussed a strong candidate. My eyes were bleary from reading applications late into the night, and my fingertips were dry from thumbing through piles of coarse paperwork. The clock on the wall read 11:07 a.m., and we still had an hour before we would break for lunch.

We thoughtfully examined each applicant. No one stood out to me in a way that sparked excitement. When the discussion about another strong candidate ended, I saw my moment to speak. "What about Aidan McHugh?" Papers rustled as my colleagues flipped through their notes.

Aidan excelled in the classroom and earned glowing recommendations. His leadership and extracurriculars stood out, even among high achievers. His passion for football practically leapt off the page. He didn't just love the game, he lived it. He dreamed of making an impact on our team.

Given the talent on our roster, I wasn't sure he'd ever be our starting quarterback. But there was a presence, a humility, and a grit about him that couldn't be measured on tape.

If he were admitted, Aidan would need a full financial aid grant to attend Peddie. That reality raised the stakes and deepened my conviction that we had to find a way to bring him here.

Although Aidan was deserving, the applicant pool was incredibly competitive. Every decision carried weight. But Aidan had demonstrated extraordinary academic aptitude, leadership potential, and the kind of heart and drive that couldn't be measured on paper. It wasn't just about test scores or grades, it was about the intangible qualities that make someone truly remarkable. And Aidan had those in spades.

As the dialogue continued, I became convinced Aidan was the right choice. I decided at that moment to fight for him. I believed he belonged at Peddie—not just for what he could gain, but for what he could give.

After a lengthy discussion, the admissions team decided to admit him and award him the Armellino Scholarship. Our director gave me the privilege of delivering the news.

I'll never forget that call. When I told Aidan he had been awarded the scholarship, he broke down in tears, overwhelmed with gratitude. His emotion caught me off guard, and before I knew it, I was crying, too. That moment solidified the emotional connection I already felt with him. It wasn't about football anymore, it was about believing in someone who had the heart and determination to make the most of an opportunity that many only dream of.

Over time, as I got to know him on and off the field, it became clear: Aidan had more heart and drive than anyone I had ever coached. He didn't have all the natural talent in the world, but what he lacked in raw skill, he more than made up for in grit, work ethic, and resilience.

I saw immense potential in him, but I was also incredibly tough on him. Not because I doubted him. Quite the opposite. I believed in him so deeply that I refused to let him settle for anything less than what I knew he could become. As a coach, my philosophy has always been simple: Love your players fiercely but push them right to the edge of what they're capable of. Aidan was no exception.

A year after that tearful phone call, as the football staff and I reviewed each player in our roster meeting, Aidan's name prompted a pause. The kind of pause that often settles over a room when tough decisions are on the horizon.

Breaking the silence, one of the coaches—a large, barrel-chested man whose commanding presence and well-earned respect gave weight to everything he said—spoke up. "This young man won't be able to help us win," he said, his tone uncharacteristically dismissive. "How important is he to discuss?"

The room fell silent again. The question lingered, its implications unfolding in the stillness. It wasn't just about the player; it was about the values we were building our program upon. What makes someone important? How do we measure their value?

Due to my difficult experience in college, I was passionate about this topic. But before I could say a word, Frankie intervened. Seated at the head of the staff table—where the head coach would normally sit, but where his chair fit best—Frankie raised his arms in the air, waved with urgency, and let out a low groan that demanded our attention.

The room fell silent as he began typing furiously on his alphabet board, his hand painstakingly pointing to each letter.

"E-V-E-R-Y-O-N-E M-A-T-T-E-R-S," he spelled out. Our newest member of the coaching staff had just stood up to one of the most respected voices in the room.

We were stunned. Frankie's words cut straight to the heart of the matter. Every young man on our roster mattered, regardless of his athletic ability. His value wasn't tied to what he could do for us on the field but to who he was as a person.

In that moment, Frankie's wisdom challenged us to reevaluate our perspective. The question wasn't whether this player could help us win games, but rather how we could help him see his worth. How could we guide him to grow into the best version of himself? And, perhaps just as importantly, how could we uncover his unique role in strengthening the team—not just on the field, but in the fabric of the program itself?

> *I'll never forget that meeting, how Frankie spoke his mind with such honesty and conviction. It wasn't just impactful for Aidan, it was a turning point for Frankie and for all of us on the coaching staff. That moment changed the way we saw Frankie and set the tone for how we would interact with him moving forward.*
>
> *I give Coach Malleo so much credit for letting it unfold naturally. He didn't force it or make it feel staged, he just created an environment where moments like that could happen organically. That was the culture he built. It wasn't about rigid rules or control; it was about trust, respect, and giving people the space to rise to the occasion.*
>
> *Looking back, that meeting was a pivotal moment for Coach Kineavy. It allowed him to establish his role in a way that felt authentic and gave us the chance to truly embrace him as part of the team. It was more than a meeting, it was a testament to what happens when leadership is grounded in connection and humility. Being part of that moment was something truly special.*

Josh Holsopple
WRs Coach
Peddie Football (2014–2019)

Aidan, who had originally been written off because his talent hadn't yet caught up with his heart and drive, became a focus of our development efforts. He wasn't the flashiest player, nor one most coaches gravitate toward. But there was something undeniable about him—a spark, a grit, a refusal to quit. We made a conscious choice to pour into him, to see beyond what he was and focus on what he could become.

After the meeting, Frankie and I lingered. "I'm sorry," he wrote, "but we should never underestimate anyone."

"We are all significant."

Frankie didn't just preach significance, he lived it. In a world quick to define people by what they lack, Frankie showed us what it meant to lead with courage, wisdom, and quiet strength. When we fail to see the innate value in others, we limit not just them but ourselves. We miss the chance to learn, grow, and be part of something greater. Ask yourself if you are valuing others for who they are or measuring their worth solely by their performance and the benefit they bring you. If your leadership is tied only to outcomes, you never unlock the potential within those you lead or within yourself.

The greatest leaders in the world don't just see people as they are, they see them as they could be. They recognize value where others don't and invest in that potential. Leadership isn't about where someone is, it's about who they can become.

That moment with Aidan reminded me of something I'd read in *Extreme Ownership* by Jocko Willink, a former Navy SEAL. During a grueling SEAL training exercise, teams of candidates were tasked with paddling heavy boats through treacherous waters. One team consistently finished last, struggling to function as a unit. Meanwhile, another team excelled, winning every race with apparent ease.

The instructors decided to swap the leaders of the two teams. The results were remarkable. The once-struggling team, under the guidance of the new leader, began winning races. What had changed? It wasn't their strength or talent. The physical capabilities of both teams remained the same. It was the *leadership*. The new leader inspired them to rise, to see their potential, and to believe they could succeed.

Great leaders elevate those around them. They don't fixate on current limitations; they look beyond them, creating a vision of what's possible and empowering people to reach it. Where doubt exists, they instill belief and unlock performance that people may not have seen in themselves.

It's easy to admire a masterpiece hanging in a gallery, but the true magic lies in the artist's ability to see beauty in a blank canvas. Great leaders are like those artists. They have the vision and courage to see what's possible before anyone else does.

It's not just about football, or even leadership. This ability to see beyond the surface is life-changing. It calls people into something higher, something they may not yet believe they can reach. When you show up as a leader who values significance over mere utility, you're not just inspiring better results, you're shaping better people, better teams, and a better world.

> It's easy to admire a masterpiece hanging in a gallery, but the true magic lies in the artist's ability to see beauty in a blank canvas.

But before we can lead others like that, we have to ask something harder: Can we see that same significance in ourselves?

The world is undeniably noisy, filled with voices eager to define your worth. But significance isn't, and has never been, determined by what others say. It is something innate, something only the individual can fully embrace.

In today's world, this wisdom is more relevant than ever. Social media, twenty-four-hour news, and endless commentary have built a world where noise often drowns out truth and volume replaces wisdom. The clamor is continuous, and it can feel overwhelming. But not all opinions deserve your attention, let alone your energy.

How often do we give credence to voices who have no place in our story? The talking heads on TV, the faceless critics on social media, and even well-meaning but misguided family members are all eager to offer their judgments. Their opinions may be loud, but they don't have to be defining.

Frankie understands this better than most. He knows that plenty of small-minded people will try to limit the significance of the life you were born to lead. They will project their fears, insecurities, and narrow perspectives onto you, attempting to convince you that your dreams are unrealistic, your values misplaced, and your efforts hopeless.

But here's the powerful truth: Their opinions only have as much power as you give them.

Frankie's wisdom isn't about dismissing others, it's about discernment. It's knowing what deserves your focus and what doesn't. Every person matters, but not every perspective aligns with your purpose, values, or vision for your life. The more energy you spend entertaining the wrong opinions, the less you have to pursue the impact you're uniquely meant to make.

That's not just idealism, it's history. We see it in every person who dared to ignore the doubters and pressed forward with courage.

Wilma Rudolph was told she might never walk again after contracting polio as a child. But she pushed through years of therapy, pain, and dismissal, eventually becoming the fastest woman in the world and winning three Olympic gold medals. She didn't let the noise of limitation define her. She trusted her own vision of what was possible.

James Dyson built over five thousand failed prototypes before launching his first successful vacuum cleaner. He spent years being rejected, dismissed, and told his idea wouldn't work. But he held onto his belief that there was a better way and eventually revolutionized an entire industry.

Natsuko Shoji, a Japanese pastry chef, began her career as a teenage apprentice, often underestimated in a male-dominated world. Instead of shrinking back, she infused fashion and art into her pastry work, turning cakes into couture. Today, she's one of the most awarded chefs in Asia—proving that originality and quiet persistence can reshape an entire craft.

What if these people had listened to the noise? What if they had let fear or criticism drown out their purpose? Instead, they trusted the voice within, the belief they mattered and their contributions could make a difference.

This isn't arrogance. It's conviction. It's the internal voice that reminds you, even in your most insecure moments, that you are significant. That your life has value and meaning.

The symphony of your life is waiting to be composed, but it requires you to tune out the noise and trust the music inside you. You don't need the world's validation to create something extraordinary. You simply need the courage to listen to yourself and to believe in your own significance.

But this is about more than just your journey. The world is desperate for leaders who understand this truth, leaders who not only trust in their own significance but also see it in others. The greatest leaders don't just make others follow; they make others feel seen, valued, and capable of greatness.

The world is full of opinions, expectations, and pressure to measure up. But in the end, significance isn't something you earn. It's something you claim.

So ask yourself: Am I letting the wrong voices define my worth? Am I measuring myself—or others—by the scoreboard or by something deeper?

Frankie didn't walk. He didn't speak. But he moved people. Because he showed up fully and unapologetically as himself. And in doing so, he helped others do the same.

The world doesn't need more people chasing applause. It needs more people rooted in purpose.

So here's your call to action: Tune out the noise. Trust the quiet music within you. And lead in a way that helps others hear theirs. Because your significance isn't just real, it's irreplaceable. And when you embrace it, you give others permission to do the same.

POWERFUL WAYS TO RECOGNIZE SIGNIFICANCE IN YOURSELF AND OTHERS

ACKNOWLEDGE YOUR UNIQUE PURPOSE

Each person has a distinct role in the larger story of life. Take time to reflect on the ways you contribute, big or small. Ask yourself: What am I uniquely equipped to offer? How do my actions create meaning for myself and others? Recognizing your purpose and the purpose of those around you cultivates a deep sense of significance.

FOCUS ON CONTRIBUTIONS, NOT COMPARISONS

Significance isn't about measuring up to others—it's about recognizing the value of what you bring to the table. Instead of comparing yourself to those around you, focus on how your unique skills, efforts, and qualities make a difference. Similarly, look at others through the lens of their contributions, appreciating what they offer without the need to rank or compare.

LISTEN DEEPLY TO UNDERSTAND

Giving someone your full attention shows them they matter. Ask open-ended questions and listen without judgment. When people feel heard, their significance is affirmed. Apply this practice to yourself, too. Listen to your inner voice, acknowledging your own hopes, dreams, and accomplishments. Be as intentional with yourself as you are with others.

RECOGNIZE THE RIPPLE EFFECT

Every action, no matter how small, can create a chain reaction of impact. A kind word, a thoughtful gesture, or a moment of encouragement can change someone's day—or life. Reflect on how your actions, even the ones that seem insignificant, contribute to the lives of others. Likewise, take a moment to see how others' actions have rippled into your life.

By focusing on contributions, listening to understand, and valuing the unique strengths of yourself and others, you can create a mindset that celebrates the significance inherent in everyone.

IN THE WORDS OF THOSE WHO LIVED IT

I arrived at The Peddie School as a poor kid from Philadelphia carrying the weight of my father's incarceration on my shoulders. Life had taught me to keep my guard up, but everything changed when I met Coach Malleo. In him, I found more than a coach, I found a leader, a father figure, and an extraordinary man who changed my life in ways I could never have imagined. He didn't just teach us football; he taught us how to fight when it mattered, how to persevere, and how to believe in ourselves.

The culture Coach Malleo created for all of us was unlike anything I've ever experienced since. It wasn't just about winning games, it was about building men of character, integrity, and resilience. When Coach Kineavy joined the staff, everything we were working toward was amplified. If Coach Malleo was the fire, then Coach Kineavy was the gasoline that made it burn even brighter. Their friendship, their bond, it was inspiring for all of us. They showed us what true leadership and teamwork looked like, not just through their words but through their actions every single day.

The stories in this book are all real. And as someone who had the honor of being coached by these two incredible men, I can tell you without hesitation there isn't a single one of us who played for this program whose heart and soul weren't touched by both of them.

This program didn't just change my trajectory, it changed who I am. Coach Malleo and Coach Kineavy didn't just make me a better player; they made me a better person. And for that, I'll always be grateful.

Keshon Farmer
RB/Captain
Peddie Football (2014–2016)
Franklin & Marshall '20
Owner, Second Chance Express

LESSON 2

Be Curious

> There is no better catalyst
> for success than curiosity.
> —MICHAEL DELL

THE SUMMER LEADING INTO MY SOPHOMORE YEAR IN COLLEGE, I
found myself sitting in a high-rise office in downtown Chicago, ner-
vously waiting for a Merrill Lynch internship interview to begin.
The view overlooked the river, the furniture gleamed, and the man
who sat across from me was everything I thought I wanted to become—polished, successful, and passionately obsessed with financial
analytics.

The problem? I was already bored.

As he talked, my eyes drifted to the bookshelf behind him. Dozens
of titles on economics and finance lined the shelves, but one stood
out: *Moneyball*. It looked completely out of place, like someone had
snuck a sports biography into a Wall Street shrine.

"See something you like?" he asked, catching me mid-stare.

"That one looks interesting," I replied, pointing.

He smiled, pulled it off the shelf, and handed it to me. "Take it,"
he said. "You'll learn more from that than you ever will interning
here." I wasn't sure whether to be grateful or offended, but I took it

anyway. I opened the book somewhere between Addison Station and the Evanston suburbs, expecting to skim a few pages. But I didn't skim. I devoured it.

Page after page, I felt the familiar thrill of finding a truth you didn't know you were searching for. I wasn't just reading a story, I was being challenged. And somewhere between chapters, I started to see the world—and my future—differently.

Moneyball was more than a story about baseball, it was a case study in curiosity-fueled leadership. Billy Beane, the general manager of the Oakland A's, had everything stacked against him: a fraction of the payroll of wealthier teams, a system rooted in outdated tradition, and a staff of scouts who judged players by how they looked in a uniform. But Beane didn't accept those limitations. He asked better questions. He challenged every assumption. He partnered with a Harvard statistician and built a team around data instead of hype; around performance, not pedigree.

> I felt the familiar thrill of finding a truth you didn't know you were searching for.

The result? In 2002, the A's won twenty straight games and made the playoffs on one of the smallest budgets in baseball. They didn't win the World Series, but they changed the game.

I became enthralled with Beane. His brashness. His willingness to zig when the world said zag. He didn't care what people thought. He cared about the truth and about finding a better way.

That story didn't just influence me. It shaped me.

To this day, *Moneyball* still runs in the background of how I approach decisions. It helped me question assumptions, listen more closely to my gut, and move past appearances to find value where others overlook it. It played a role in why I hired Frankie.

I've learned that leadership sometimes means seeking consensus and sometimes means silencing the noise to trust your own convictions. These decisions often carry the most weight, not because they're easy or universally supported, but because they demand a deep trust in your own instincts and the courage to live with the consequences. The clarity that comes from knowing the decision is yours alone makes it easier to stand by it no matter what the outcome.

When I was still finding my footing as a head football coach, I leaned heavily on collaboration, relying on the perspectives of my staff to guide decisions for the program. That democratic approach is an essential part of my leadership philosophy. But when it came to hiring Frankie, I didn't ask for anyone's opinion. I didn't call a meeting, weigh the pros and cons, or debate his fit with the team. After spending two hours with Frankie, I didn't need to.

In that room, something shifted inside me. I left our meeting with a conviction I had rarely felt before, a certainty that hiring him was the right decision, no matter the questions, challenges, or doubts. I couldn't fully explain it, but I knew it. Frankie didn't walk in with fanfare or flash, but somehow the room felt warmer with him in it. The way he looked you in the eye, the calm in his posture, it was like gravity bent gently toward him. I saw something extraordinary in him—something the world needed to see—and I trusted he would bring a value to our team no one else could.

This wasn't just a hire; it was a statement to myself and to my team. It was a moment when I chose to lead with conviction, not consensus. I didn't know what the outcome would be. I didn't know how Frankie would be received or how his role would evolve. But I knew if I trusted myself and my instincts, I could live with the results, good or bad, without regret.

Leadership isn't always about certainty. More often, it's about faith, faith in yourself, faith in the potential of things you cannot yet see, and, in my case, faith in God's guidance when the path ahead feels unclear. Hiring Frankie wasn't just about giving him a chance; it was about listening to a deeper calling, a conviction placed in my heart that this decision was part of something far greater. I didn't see Frankie's presence as a risk; I saw it as an opportunity, an opportunity for growth, and for God to work through us both. I believe God uses unlikely circumstances and unexpected people to reveal his greater purpose. Frankie was one of those people.

After officially hiring Frankie and introducing him to our coaching staff, it was time to introduce him to our team. I scheduled a team meeting before winter break, a touchpoint to set expectations for the offseason workout program and to welcome Frankie into the program.

If you've never been in a football team room, it's hard to describe the sheer energy and chaos that fills the air before a meeting begins. Especially at the end of a long school day, the space is alive with bravado, laughter, and the sounds of restless teenage boys letting off steam. On this day, the atmosphere was no different. The players were alive with excitement of exams ending and winter break starting.

Within our football program, we had a unique tradition of communication we called "three claps." At the end of every meeting, players and coaches alike would clap three times in unison as a ritual of unity, purpose, and respect. Anyone could initiate three claps, and when they did, the entire program responded without hesitation. It was never done frivolously. For us, those three claps were a way to signal approval or show respect. Guest speakers addressing the team were often met with three thunderous claps instead of the obligatory applause, making the moment feel intentional and meaningful.

As was the standard with every new coach I hired, I planned to formally introduce Frankie during this meeting. I wanted to ensure he was welcomed as an equal member of our staff. On the day of the meeting, I could hear the familiar hum of voices echoing through the halls as I approached the team room. The energy was palpable.

But today's introduction wasn't just about adding a coach. It was about shifting our values.

Our football team meetings were held in the Caspersen History House, or simply "Caspersen" as it was affectionately called by the Peddie community. With its tiered auditorium seating and massive media screen, it was the ideal space to address the team and break down game film.

The building bore the name of Finn M.W. Caspersen Sr., a distinguished Peddie alum, renowned philanthropist, and former CEO of Beneficial Corporation. His legacy was unmistakable. As you entered, his portrait greeted you with an unrelenting gaze, its presence impossible to ignore. There was a gravity to it, an unspoken expectation that seemed to bleed through the brushstrokes. It was as if he was watching, silently reminding all who passed through those doors of the standards they were meant to uphold.

Most of our staff had already taken their seats in the team room, mingling with players as I approached the doors that separated the room from the hallway. Frankie was waiting patiently, his hands resting lightly on the controls of his wheelchair. "Are you ready to meet the team?" I asked.

He nodded firmly, his expression calm and composed. I pulled open the heavy wooden door, its hinges letting out a long squeak. Stepping aside, I held the door and motioned for Frankie to enter first.

As soon as he rolled through the doorway, the wave of noise that had been spilling into the hallway abruptly stopped. Frankie, with the deft touch of a Formula 1 driver, navigated to the center of the room with me in tow. Players, seated in tiered rows above us, looked down as we came to a stop.

The sunlight streaming through the all-glass backdrop of Caspersen cast a dazzling glow, making it hard to discern every expression. Still, I caught flickers of curiosity, subtle glances exchanged between teammates, and the lingering uncertainty etched in their movements. I couldn't blame them. For most of these young men, it was likely their first encounter with someone who navigated life like Frankie.

"Good afternoon," I began. "This is Frankie Kineavy. He will be joining our coaching staff."

I gave a brief background on Frankie, shared that he would serve as our director of football operations, as well as assistant linebackers coach, and closed by telling the team that he would be referred to as Coach Kineavy moving forward.

I turned to Frankie. "Coach Kineavy, would you like to address the team?"

He nodded, and the room grew still as Frankie began to type on his alphabet board. His clenched hand moved with effort and precision, spelling out his message one arduous letter at a time. It took a moment—long enough for the implications of his effort to settle over the room.

I leaned in and read it aloud: "I am excited to get to know all of you."

At face value, the words seemed simple, even ordinary. Most people might have brushed them off as a polite platitude or a phrase you say because it's expected. But coming from Frankie, those words carried a heaviness that went far beyond their surface.

Frankie didn't have the luxury of filler. Every single letter, every word he chose, came at a cost, each one requiring focus, effort, and time. For him, communicating was never easy, and that difficulty gave his words a rare significance. He didn't waste letters. If he was saying something, it mattered.

In that moment, the players understood that Frankie wasn't offering small talk; he was offering a connection. He wasn't there to impress them or command the room; he was there to know them. His words weren't rehearsed or obligatory; they were deliberate and full of meaning. The players felt it.

What could have been dismissed as a throwaway phrase became something more. It became a testament to his sincerity, his curiosity, and his intention to truly see and understand each player in the room. "Thank you, Coach Kineavy," I said, nodding in acknowledgment.

Just as Frankie began to turn his wheelchair to leave the center of the room to take his place with the other coaches, a voice suddenly boomed from the back: "Three claps!"

In unison and without hesitation the entire room responded. *CLAP. CLAP. CLAP.*

The sound echoed through Caspersen, through the hall, through every preconception that had walked into that room with us.

Frankie didn't demand their respect. He earned it without ever raising his voice, his hand, or his stature. Just by being exactly who he was.

The day Coach Malleo introduced Coach Kineavy to the team stands out vividly. None of us knew what to expect, but the second Coach Kineavy started typing, the room was completely locked in. You could feel the weight of the moment. The three claps were powerful. If you were ever in a Coach Malleo-led meeting, the three claps meant something. That day, someone in the back shouted "three claps" and the entire team was locked in. It was like a wave of energy passed through us. The hair on my arms stood straight up, and even now when I think about it I get the same chills.

I was fortunate to play for Coach Dabo Swinney, who I consider the greatest leader and motivator in college football. Looking back, I realize Coach Malleo was like a preview of the kind of leadership I'd later see in Coach Swinney. The way he commanded a room, the energy he brought, and the way he spoke to us—not just as players but as young men—was on another level. For a high school coach to lead with that kind of presence was unheard of. He didn't just coach us, he inspired us to become something greater.

Coach Kineavy was an inspiration to all of us. His presence that day wasn't just powerful; it was life-altering. But what made that moment possible was Coach Malleo. He had a way of creating those experiences, of setting the stage for us to grow not just as athletes but as people. That meeting was one of many where Coach Malleo and Coach Kineavy taught us what it means to lead, to inspire, and to strive for something bigger than ourselves.

Noah Dehond
OL/Captain
Peddie Football (2014–2016)
LT, Clemson University Football, '20
2018 National Champion

Though I didn't realize it at the time, that moment set the tone for what was to come over the next four years.

In the early days of our coaching journey together, I unconsciously fell into the trap of trying to "compensate" for Frankie. I planned around what I assumed might be challenges, thinking I'd need to carry more of the responsibilities or shield him from tasks that seemed overly demanding. But Frankie didn't have time for pity or assumptions. From day one, he shattered both.

One evening, we were breaking down film after a particularly tough game. We had played sloppy in victory, and the film didn't lie; missed assignments, lazy technique, and mental errors were evident. The atmosphere in the room was tense. A few coaches sat hunched over their laptops, others leaned back in silence, replaying moments in their heads. Frankie sat at the end of the table, quietly watching.

I assumed I'd have to carry the discussion or simplify it for him. But before I could even begin, Frankie pointed—slowly, deliberately—to a sequence on the screen.

It was a third-and-short in the second quarter. Our linebacker had misread the formation, hesitated, and shot the wrong gap, turning a routine stop into a twelve-yard gain. It hadn't been glaring in real time, but on film it was obvious.

Frankie spelled out his comment on his board, pausing only briefly between letters.

L-I-N-E-B-A-C-K-E-R W-A-S L-A-T-E T-O R-E-A-D.

We all turned toward him. Then back to the screen. He was right.

It was the kind of detailed observation you'd expect from a veteran coach, not someone who'd spent the entire game in a wheelchair on the sideline, communicating one letter at a time. But that's who Frankie was. Sharp. Focused. Quietly commanding the room.

At that moment, something clicked for me. Frankie wasn't there to be a participant in name only, and he wasn't there to inspire simply by his presence. He was there to lead. To elevate us. To teach us to look deeper—not just at the game, but at ourselves and each other.

True leadership isn't about authority or titles. It's about uncovering and nurturing the potential that lies beneath the surface. It's about looking past assumptions, past appearances, and seeing the extraordinary in people that others might overlook.

Frankie wasn't just a coach. Or an advisor. He was living proof that deep wisdom and quiet strength often hide in the places we dismiss too quickly.

The players, too, began to learn this lesson. At first, many were unsure how to interact with Frankie. Some hesitated to speak directly to him, worried they might say the wrong thing or unsure how to interpret his responses. There was a natural awkwardness in those early days as they tried to navigate the unfamiliar.

But it didn't take long for them to see past the alphabet board, the chair, and the movements they didn't fully understand. Frankie's sharp wit, his focus on their growth, and his genuine ability to connect broke through any barriers.

Before long, he was simply "Coach Kineavy"—someone they trusted, someone they listened to, and someone they deeply respected. His presence became less about what he couldn't do and entirely about what he brought to the team: insight, compassion, and belief in their potential.

I learned through working with Frankie to ask questions before making assumptions about a person. What's their story? What do they bring to the table? What strengths or perspectives might I be overlooking? Those simple yet profound questions changed the way I lead, the way I parent, and the way I approach every interaction. They shifted my focus from judgment to curiosity, from assumptions to understanding.

By the end of the first season, that shift was embedded in our team's culture. Players became more supportive of one another, more willing to take risks, and more intentional in their connections. They saw each other not as competitors or rivals but as teammates united by mutual respect, shared purpose, and the belief that everyone brought something valuable to the equation.

Frankie wasn't just part of the team; he was its heart. And the way he lives, refusing to be defined by appearances or assumptions, became a model for all of us.

The world is full of people whose potential is overlooked because of snap judgments and surface assumptions. But Frankie taught me that the most extraordinary stories often lie just beneath the surface—quiet, unassuming, and waiting to be discovered.

There's a moment in the hit TV series *Ted Lasso* where the title character says, "Be curious, not judgmental." It's simple, but powerful. Judgment closes doors. Curiosity opens them. And when you lead with curiosity, you don't just learn about others, you invite them to become their best.

If I had judged Frankie by appearance alone, I might have missed everything he brought to our team. To me. To my family. That thought still humbles me. His insight, humor, wisdom, and grit impacted us in ways I couldn't have scripted—but desperately needed.

Frankie taught me to look deeper. To ask more. To see what others miss. And to never underestimate the quiet strength of someone who leads with presence instead of noise.

In the end, the best leaders aren't the loudest in the room. They're the ones who make others feel seen. Who ask rather than assume. Who listen more than they speak.

That's the legacy Frankie created—not in game plans or playbooks, but in the way we saw each other.

So look again. Look closer. There's greatness hiding in someone you've dismissed.

And if you're not careful, you might miss it in yourself, too.

POWERFUL WAYS TO BE CURIOUS, NOT JUDGMENTAL

ASK OPEN-ENDED QUESTIONS

When faced with uncertainty or unfamiliarity, replace judgment with curiosity by asking open-ended questions. Instead of assuming you know someone's intentions or story, ask, "Can you tell me more about that?" or "What inspired you to make that choice?" These questions invite dialogue, deepen understanding, and build connections.

CHALLENGE YOUR ASSUMPTIONS

Pay attention to moments when you find yourself jumping to conclusions. Pause and ask yourself, "What evidence do I have for this belief?" or "What might I be missing?" By challenging your assumptions, you open the door to seeing things from a new perspective.

FOCUS ON LISTENING, NOT REACTING

In conversations, prioritize listening with the intent to understand rather than to respond. Practice active listening by maintaining eye contact, nodding, and summarizing what the other person says before sharing your own thoughts. This approach demonstrates respect and genuine interest, fostering trust and openness.

ADOPT A LEARNER'S MINDSET

Approach situations and people as opportunities to learn. Instead of judging someone's differences, ask yourself, "What can I glean from this person's experience?" or "How can this situation broaden my perspective?" Viewing life through the lens of curiosity turns challenges into growth opportunities.

IN THE WORDS OF THOSE WHO LIVED IT

My time at Peddie was truly inspiring. While the school is renowned for its academic rigor, it was the football program led by Coach Malleo, with the support of Coach Kineavy, that left an indelible mark on my life. Their culture rivaled that of any elite program, including Notre Dame, where I now play. Coach Malleo's leadership fostered an ultra-competitive environment where personal improvement was always in service of the team's success.

One of the most impactful lessons was the standard of excellence Coach Malleo instilled. His mantra, "No one cleans up after Peddie football," taught us humility and accountability, while "If you're not fifteen minutes early, you're late" reinforced discipline and preparation. These principles became cornerstones of our team and my life. Coach Malleo lives these values, inspiring us with his work ethic and belief in going beyond what's expected. His favorite saying, "Event + Response = Outcome," became a guiding principle, teaching us to focus on our response to any challenge.

Coach Kineavy exemplified resilience and dedication. Despite his physical limitations, he was present at every practice, meeting, and game, showing us that strength is found in perseverance. His determination and innovative approach to coaching reminded us to never take opportunities for granted and to always give our best.

Together, Coach Malleo and Coach Kineavy demanded and modeled excellence, shaping us into better athletes and, more importantly, better men. They taught us to approach life with gratitude, respect, and a commitment to finish every task with the same intensity we started. Their influence extended far beyond the field, leaving a lasting impact on all of us.

To this day, I carry their lessons with me. "Excellence is the standard" wasn't just a motto; it was a way of life. Coach Malleo and Coach Kineavy weren't just incredible football coaches, they were leaders whose vision and dedication shaped the lives of everyone they touched, including mine.

Davis Sherwood
LB/TE/Captain, Peddie Football (2017–2019)
TE/FB, Notre Dame Football, '24
Author: *Woody: What Would Woody Do?*

The Only Disability
Is a Bad Attitude

> When you arise in the morning,
> think of what a privilege it is to be alive—
> to breathe, to think, to enjoy, to love.
> —MARCUS AURELIUS

YEARS BEFORE I HIRED FRANKIE—back when I was just a high school kid with a one-track mind and a chip on my shoulder—someone else gave me a lesson in attitude I didn't see coming.

It was the summer before my senior year, and the August heat in Wall Township, New Jersey, was the kind that pressed down on you like a second skin. The air was heavy, thick with humidity, and everything around me seemed to shimmer in the late-afternoon sun. I was out running hill sprints in my neighborhood—my version of a summer break. No crowd, no coach, just me and the pavement, chasing something only I could see.

By the time I finished my last sprint, sweat was pouring off me. My legs burned, my lungs ached, and every part of me wanted to collapse. But instead, I jogged down the street, easing my pace as I approached home.

Our house sat high up on a hill, tucked into one of the quieter corners of town where meandering driveways unfolded beneath shade trees and American flags flapped gently from front porches. Our driveway was long and steep, making snow shoveling a nightmare and a trip to the curbside mailbox a cross-country trek.

I slowed to a walk as I approached the mailbox, chest still heaving. The door hung slightly ajar, a few envelopes peeking out. Bills. Junk mail. And one envelope with the school crest printed in the corner. My senior-year schedule.

I ripped it open right there, sweat dripping onto the page. Most of it looked routine—until one line stopped me in my tracks: Mr. Johnson. English IV.

If you had asked me back then to list the strengths of my high school experience, "intellectual curiosity" wouldn't have cracked the top ten. I was bright but academically unmotivated. School came easy, which made it easy to coast. I had convinced myself it was cooler to do the bare minimum than to excel.

My entire identity was tethered to football—my singular obsession and, in my mind, my ticket to college.

While my classmates partied or explored newfound freedom, I was alone in the stadium at night, running stair after stair until my legs gave out. I'd position my parents' car so the headlights lit up the concrete steps, carving a path through the darkness. Drenched in sweat, heart pounding, I pushed myself constantly because I believed every drop of effort was proof that I was destined for something bigger.

Football wasn't just a sport, it was my reason, my anchor, my identity. It consumed me. It eclipsed everything else.

And yet, despite my indifference toward academics, I built some powerful relationships with teachers. One of them broke through in a way I never expected.

Mr. Jim Johnson.

He was young, charismatic, and carried himself with the quiet confidence of someone who knew exactly who he was. A father of two, he balanced firm guidance with genuine connection. When he spoke to you, it felt like you were the only person in the room—a rare gift that made every conversation meaningful.

He'd been my basketball coach during freshman year. But unlike any coach I'd ever had, he didn't just push us to win. He challenged us to think. To reflect. To lead. Pep talks turned into mini life lessons. Sometimes they were wrapped in poetry. Other times, in dead silence, followed by a single question that stuck with us for days.

From that year on, Mr. Johnson became a constant in my life. He was a mentor who always showed up at the right moment, sometimes to lift me up and sometimes to knock me down a peg. But always with belief. Belief in who I was becoming—even when I couldn't see it yet.

And now, out of nowhere Mr. Johnson was on my schedule.

As I entered my senior year football season, I had grown from the awkward boy who had started playing football in eighth grade into the captain of one of the state's top-ranked teams. I was focused on bringing a state championship to our town, and I left no stone unturned in pursuit of that goal.

When the school year began, football remained my central focus. My life was consumed by weight room sessions, film study, and dreams of hoisting a state championship trophy. English class, in my mind, was just another box to check on the road to graduation.

On that first day, I walked into Mr. Johnson's class—a small, cramped space that felt more like an archive than a classroom. The walls were covered in posters of literary giants: Whitman, Faulkner, Hemingway, and Shakespeare stared back from their faded frames, as if daring me to care. Quotes were scrawled across the chalkboard in sweeping cursive, some of which barely registered in my quest for a seat at the back of the room. I slid into my chair, arms folded, confident I'd found the perfect vantage point to coast through the semester.

But Mr. Johnson had other plans.

He calmly entered, perched on the edge of his desk, and scanned the room. I avoided eye contact, but felt his gaze on me and looked up. A small smirk played at the corner of his mouth. "Mr. Malleo," he said, his voice firm but easy, "I'd like you to sit up here, front and center."

There was no judgment in his tone, just a quiet confidence that let me know arguing would be pointless. As I made my way to the front, I could hear some snickering. I wasn't the only person who'd hidden in the back, but apparently I would be the only one caught.

As the bell rang to end class, Mr. Johnson called me over to his desk. He waited for the room to empty out. "I know you're not living up to your potential as a student," he said evenly. There was no scolding in his tone, just quiet truth. "I've read your writing, and I know there's more in you."

Those words lodged in my mind. He liked my writing? I didn't even like my writing. Why did he believe in me so much?

I left class with more questions than answers. Mr. Johnson's words gnawed at the edges of my focus. No teacher had ever said something like that to me before—not as a challenge, not with belief.

That day, something shifted. I wondered if there was more in me, something beyond the football field, something I hadn't yet discovered.

The next day, I arrived early and took my seat at the front of the room. Mr. Johnson led us through the works of Thoreau, Joyce, and Dickinson. Their words were vivid, teeming with meaning, and Mr. Johnson infused them with life. He didn't deliver lectures from a podium. He *lived* inside the stories and poems, drawing us in with his passion and questions, connecting the material to who we were as people. He didn't just teach literature—he invited us to wrestle with it, to feel its impact, its beauty, and its relevance to our lives.

And then came the poem that changed me: "If" by Rudyard Kipling. The words reached across the page and grabbed something deep within me.

> *If you can dream—and not make dreams your master;*
> *If you can think—and not make thoughts your aim;*
> *If you can meet with Triumph and Disaster*
> *And treat those two impostors just the same.*

As I read the passage, I saw greatness not as a destination or an unreachable ideal but as a choice—one we make in how we respond to life's highs and lows. Triumph and disaster are impostors. They are fleeting yet have the power to define us—*if* we let them.

That stanza planted a seed in me. Life is not about avoiding failure or chasing perfection. It's about how we show up, how we carry ourselves, and how we choose to navigate the storms. Mr. Johnson didn't teach me to read Kipling's words; he showed me how to live them.

That day in class, I felt a flicker of something greater. Maybe greatness wasn't about touchdowns or trophies or stats. Maybe it wasn't about the applause of others or the labels they placed on us. Maybe it was about the attitude we carried—the quiet strength to keep going, to rise above both success and failure, and to never let either own us.

This perspective that our attitude is the great equalizer has become a cornerstone of how I approach life, leadership, and adversity. Challenges beyond our control will always come, often without warning. But what remains unshakably in our grasp is our response. Do we allow adversity to crush us? Do we let success lull us into complacency?

> Challenges
>
> beyond our control
>
> will always come,
>
> often without
>
> warning. But
>
> what remains
>
> unshakably in
>
> our grasp is our
>
> response.

Or do we, as Kipling so powerfully urges, stand strong, treating triumph and disaster as the fleeting charlatans they are?

"If" didn't just speak to me; it became a part of me. For years, I carried a creased, weathered copy of the poem in my wallet—its edges frayed, its words etched into my memory. It was my silent guide through moments of doubt, frustration, and success, a constant reminder to hold steady when the storms of life raged. To me, it was more than literature; it was a philosophy for living, a practical manual for facing both life's setbacks and its victories with grace, humility, and resolve.

As a coach at Peddie, I would begin every football season by gathering the team in Caspersen for our first meeting. With the expectation and promise of a new year ahead, I would recite "If." In those moments, Kipling's words became more than a poem—they became a shared declaration of who we aspired to be. Together, we committed to face every opponent, every setback, and every success with the same unflinching resolve.

Kipling's message was clear: Life is not defined by what happens to us, but by how we choose to respond. And that truth transcended football. It wasn't just about playing the game, it was about how we carried ourselves as teammates, leaders, and young men. It was about holding steady when everything around us seemed uncertain, refusing to be swayed by either failure or glory.

In reciting "If" to the team, I wasn't just sharing a poem, I was sounding a call to action. A challenge to face life head-on, embrace the journey, and become the kind of people who endure, persevere, and rise above their circumstances.

From the moment Frankie joined the staff, he became a critical part of our mission to grow the program and build the culture. Though he had only been with us a few weeks, his impact was profound. Frankie brought a unique perspective and insight that elevated everyone around him. He saw the game—and the people in it—with an unmatched clarity, his observations sharp and his insights piercing. But what truly set him apart wasn't just his intelligence or his eye for detail, it was his commitment to showing up, no matter the obstacles. Day in and day out, Frankie was there, rolling across the field, tracking drills, taking notes, and offering wisdom that far exceeded the X's and O's of the game. His commitment reminded all of us—players, coaches, and staff—that showing up matters, that effort matters, and that attitude was the bedrock of everything we did. He didn't just talk about resilience; he lived it.

During the summer of Frankie's second season on our staff, I had arranged for our team to attend a grueling full-contact camp in Virginia. The eight-hour drive alone was daunting, not to mention the sweltering July heat and the camp's complete lack of accommodations for someone with Frankie's needs. I never expected him to make the trip. In fact, I assured him more than once that his contributions were already invaluable and that no one would think less of him for sitting this one out.

But Frankie wouldn't hear of it.

With the help of his parents Frank Sr. and Madeline, Frankie booked a hotel room and made the journey. Day after day, he was there—on the sidelines, in team meetings, and at every scrimmage. While the rest of us were drenched in sweat, barking out drills, or nursing bruises, Frankie was locked in, laser-focused. He observed everything, including how we moved, how we communicated, and where we left space.

Between sessions, his meticulous notes would find their way into my hands. One day, he pointed out how our outside linebackers were crashing too early and giving up the edge. Another time, he flagged a receiver tipping his routes with his stance—something none of the other coaches had caught. And in one scrimmage, he noted that our backside safety was consistently late on run support because his pre-snap alignment was a step too deep.

These weren't just smart observations, they were difference-makers.

Frankie had a gift for seeing what others couldn't. His insights made us sharper, more intentional, and more connected as a team.

Frankie didn't miss a moment, no matter how unforgiving the weather or how unkind the terrain. He rolled himself, sometimes laboriously, across fields, through locker rooms, and into team huddles, always carrying the same quiet determination and sharp wit that reminded us to stop making excuses and start leaning into the work.

Frankie changed our coaching staff. He set a standard. His presence wasn't about convenience or comfort. It was about showing up fully and without compromise. That kind of leadership doesn't just inspire, it demands reflection. Watching him in action forced me to look inward and ask myself: *Am I showing up with this level of commitment? Am I leading with the same resolve?*

No excuses. No shortcuts. Just an unyielding belief in the mission and the people working toward it. Frankie reminded us that leadership is rarely about the words we say, it's about what we're willing to endure, sacrifice, and contribute when the conditions are far from perfect. Leadership is about showing up, period.

As that summer wore on, an unexpected opportunity presented itself: a chance to play the top-ranked parochial powerhouse in the state. Their roster was stacked with Division I talent, including recruits bound for programs like Notre Dame and Ohio State. They were so dominant, their scheduled opponent had forfeited the game, citing safety concerns. No one wanted to play them.

But when their open date aligned with ours, I didn't hesitate. Where others saw a reason to back down, we saw an opportunity to rise. Without fanfare, we booked the game, fully aware of the challenge that lay ahead. For our team, this wasn't about matching their talent or reputation, it was about proving who we were, no matter the odds.

Game day arrived, and as our small yellow bus groaned into the stadium parking lot, it felt like we were entering an ancient coliseum. The early September air was alive, thick. The stadium, though modest by most elite high school standards, had an aura that seemed to magnify its presence. On one side of the field, the bleachers rose steeply, a wall of steel and concrete looming above our sideline like a challenge. *You ready to climb this mountain?* they seemed to ask.

But it wasn't the structure itself that intimidated—it was the crowd.

The home team's student section had turned the stadium into their battleground. As the bus hissed to a stop, the swarm of students began their march toward us, a synchronized wave of chaos. They moved as one, clad in their school's maroon and silver, faces painted like warriors. Some were shirtless, their bare torsos streaked with sweat and paint; others carried random objects—a drum here, a megaphone there—brandished for no reason other than intimidation.

As we descended the bus steps, their chants bellowed like a battle cry, perfectly timed and rehearsed. It wasn't the wild, uncoordinated noise of an ordinary crowd; it was precise, deliberate. The rhythm of their songs reverberated through the parking lot, their voices unified in a way that sent shivers down your spine. It wasn't hard to imagine they had practiced this moment, over and over, waiting for us. Somewhere a drill sergeant was smiling.

I made the mistake of making eye contact with one of the boys, a maroon headband serving as the only layer of protection between his face and beads of sweat. His eyes lit up as though he had been waiting for this very moment since his science class on Monday.

That was all it took.

Like predators circling their prey, they swooped in, their voices growing louder, sharper, more pointed. Insults flew with machine-gun precision, striking everything in their path—me, our team, even the bus we had arrived in. They jeered, laughed, and shouted. It was a symphony of hostility, and we were the unwelcome guests.

It wasn't just heckling. It was psychological warfare.

If *Lord of the Flies* had a scene set in a high school football stadium, this would have been it. The football field was their island, the bleachers their domain, and we had wandered into their territory.

And I loved every minute of it.

As we took the field for warmups, rows of gleaming silver helmets lined the far sideline, catching the last rays of the setting sun. Their large pirate logo seemed to glare back at us, as if to say, *Even our logo is here to beat you.*

Forty yards away, their players moved with purpose and precision, a finely-tuned sea of Division I talent. They looked every bit the part of a team destined for greatness—perfectly polished athletes, their movements crisp and deliberate. They had more coaches on their sideline than we had players.

Their head coach stood at the center of it all, a commanding figure exuding authority like a general on a battlefield. His physique was solid, built with a no-nonsense presence that demanded respect. His neatly trimmed mustache and gray flat top seemed plucked straight from an '80s action movie, completing the aura of someone who clearly expected dominance.

By contrast, our small group of twenty-three players warmed up on the opposite side of the field. Although we were small in total roster size, our players moved with swagger that belied our numbers. They were loose, confident, and unfazed. Many bobbed their heads to the beat of Kanye West's "Power" blasting over the sound system.

I found myself caught up in the moment, bobbing my head along with them, a quiet grin spreading across my face. This was who we were—fearless, scrappy, and undeterred by the odds stacked against us.

We had created a culture that thrived on the underdog role. Our players didn't see themselves as outmatched, they saw themselves as warriors. As I walked through the warm up lines, I repeated the mantra they had come to love, my voice booming across the field: "They have many men but *few warriors!*"

The players echoed the sentiment, their voices rising with each repetition. It wasn't just a saying, it was a belief. While their roster might have dwarfed ours in numbers, they didn't have what we had: a gritty team willing to battle to the final whistle, no matter the opponent.

To the outside world, this game was already over before it began. It was David versus Goliath, an inevitable blowout waiting to happen. But remember how that matchup ended?

When I was a player, I never cared much for grandiose pregame speeches. Those were for the movies, I thought. Whatever emotional high they offered was fleeting—always secondary to technique, fundamentals, and strategy. As a coach, I carried that philosophy forward. My pregame addresses were direct and measured. I spoke with confidence, ensuring the focus was on the team, not on me. It was their moment, not mine.

Although that was normally my approach, I knew going into this game it would be different. Weeks earlier, during a staff meeting, we had discussed the challenge ahead—the enormity of what we were stepping into. This wasn't just any game. It was *the* game, a defining moment for our upstart program. I knew it called for something more. Something special. Someone special.

So, I asked Frankie to speak. And he agreed without hesitation.

Frankie understood the gravity of the moment. This wasn't just about football—it was about proving that what we were building could stand toe-to-toe with the best. He had been with us every step of the way—watching, encouraging, advising. He didn't lead drills or break down film, but his presence shaped everything. Every meeting, every rep, every ounce of effort was infused with the standard he helped set. Frankie knew what was at stake. And he knew exactly how to meet the challenge.

On select occasions, Frankie used a voice box to prerecord his thoughts. The device translated his typed words into a cold, robotic tone, and it was a stark contrast to the warmth and authenticity of the man behind them. That day, it wasn't smooth, it wasn't natural, but the words themselves, crafted with intention, every letter painstakingly chosen, were profoundly human.

Frankie didn't need a polished voice to deliver his message. He just needed a stage and a moment, and these were his.

The cramped away locker room was anything but ideal for a moment like this. Bodies were packed shoulder to shoulder, helmets clutched in hands or perched precariously on benches. Some players stood on the wooden slats to make space, their cleats thudding softly on the worn surface. The humidity of that early afternoon was unforgiving, the air filled with sweat and tension. It was as if the room itself was challenging us.

And then, Frankie began.

The mechanical voice filled the room, cutting through the stillness. The sound was foreign, cold, almost unsettling at first. But the words? The words were alive. Frankie spoke of brotherhood. He spoke of unity, of the sacrifices they had made for each other, of the hours they had spent preparing for this very moment. He reminded them that no matter what the scoreboard said at the end of the night, their success would be measured in how they showed up for one another.

And as we walked out of that stifling locker room and into the cool evening, I knew one thing for certain: We would not come back the same team that entered it.

From the opening kickoff, we were fighting not just against our opponent, but against the crowd and even the officials. Early in the game, an obvious fourth-down touchdown pass that would have tied the score at 7 was inexplicably overturned. The crowd roared in approval, while our sideline ignited in disbelief. To make matters worse, the officials granted our opponent a touchdown pass that was clearly out of bounds to make the score 14-0. The injustice was infuriating, both as a coach and as a competitor. The crowd fed off our frustration, their chants and jeers echoing into the night.

Then, Frankie called me over, motioning for a time-out. The ref's whistle pierced the air, and our team trudged toward the sideline like soldiers on their last march. One of our linemen flung his helmet to the ground. Another muttered something inaudible.

That's when Frankie started rolling forward. The artificial turf was soft from humidity, the rubber pellets clinging to his wheels. He maneuvered his way to the middle of the huddle—sweat dripping from players' brows, eyes locked on him. He typed on his board. I read it aloud: "You don't have to win this game. You just have to love playing it."

The silence cracked. A grin. Then a laugh. Helmets went back on. Shoulders lifted. One of the players yelled, "Let's go!"

And just like that, we were alive again.

On the next offensive series, our players took the field with renewed energy. A long drive ended with a touchdown, cutting the deficit to 24-7 as we headed into halftime.

The locker room buzzed with a strange mix of tension and optimism. The air was damp with sweat, the smell of grass and adrenaline mingling with the metallic tang of athletic tape. Players sat slumped on benches, chugging water, their breaths coming in sharp, heavy gasps. Jerseys clung to their backs.

I stood in the center of the room, the fluorescent lights flickering slightly. Around me, coaches were mapping out adjustments on whiteboards, their voices blending with the sounds of exhaustion and determination. Frankie, sitting to the side with his ever-present calm, scanned the room, typing occasional notes of encouragement.

"We're not out of this," I said, raising my voice above the murmurs. "We've been here before. They're bigger, stronger, but they're not tougher. And they don't have what we have: heart. Go out there and play for each other."

Frankie typed something, and I read it aloud: "One play at a time. Have fun." The boys cheered, slapping pads and helmets, filling the room with a newfound energy.

The second half started with a jolt. We returned the kickoff for a touchdown, cutting the lead to 24-14. The roar from our sideline was deafening. Now we had a ball game.

They answered with another touchdown to make it 31-14, but our team refused to back down. Despite being outnumbered and overmatched, we clawed our way back. A long drive ended with another touchdown, though a missed extra point left us trailing 31-20.

On their next possession, our defense dug deep. With sheer grit and determination, they stopped the opponent on a critical fourth down.

The sideline was filled with energy, players and coaches jumping and shouting. The momentum had shifted.

A few plays later, we scored again, but our two-point conversion attempt failed. The score stood at 31–26 early in the fourth quarter.

I glanced at our players, many of whom were bending over, hands on their knees, sucking in air. The sheer size and strength of our opponent were beginning to wear us down. Their coaches rotated in fresh bodies for offense, defense, and special teams. Most of our boys never left the field.

Still, they fought.

After our touchdown, the pressure shifted squarely onto our opponent. They felt it. On their next possession, they threw an interception, and our sideline exploded in celebration. Helmets flew into the air, players screamed, and I grabbed my clipboard, knowing this was our chance. We had the number one team in the state on the ropes ready to throw the knockout blow.

We called one of our favorite plays, King Left Purple 32 Jumpman, a double-post concept designed to get the ball into the hands of our best player. He was an incredible athlete who is now in the NFL, the kind of kid who could leap over defenders and carry a team on his back. He was the reason we were even in the game.

The ball spiraled through the night air, cutting against the stadium lights as he broke free down the field. It was a perfect throw, a moment that seemed destined for glory.

And then, he dropped it.

The ball slipped through his hands, falling to the turf like a stone. The stadium went silent, and I could feel the air being sucked from our sideline. The boys hung their heads, and even the crowd seemed to hesitate, unsure of how to react. Moments later, we were forced to punt.

With our worn-down team on the field, the inevitable happened. Their offense pounded the ball downfield, taking advantage of our exhaustion. A few plays later, they punched it into the end zone, sealing the game with a final score that didn't reflect the heart and fight we had shown.

The final whistle blew, and the game was over. As the players lined up to shake hands, I walked toward the opposing coach, my heart heavy but my head held high. He extended his hand, but as I reached for it, he pulled me into an embrace.

"I've never seen a team play with such heart and passion," he said, his voice filled with sincerity. For a moment, the loss felt lighter, his words cutting through the sting of defeat like a cool breeze.

As we exited the field, eyes up despite the outcome, something extraordinary happened. The same opposing student section that had greeted us with heckling and intimidation now rose to their feet. At first, it was just a few scattered claps, hesitant and almost uncertain, but then it grew. The applause swelled, wave after wave, until the entire section was on its feet clapping in admiration.

I stopped in my tracks, turning to look at them, trying to process what was happening. It wasn't jeers or mockery—it was genuine respect.

Many of them had removed their caps, tipping them toward us in a gesture of approval.

The players noticed it, too. As they walked off the field, defeated but unbroken, they glanced toward the stands, some nodding, others offering small waves of acknowledgment. Their exhaustion was on display, but so was their pride.

In that moment, the sting of the loss faded into the background. We had accomplished something that couldn't be captured on a scoreboard. We had earned their respect—not just as competitors, but as a team that refused to quit, a team that played with heart and soul.

Later, in the post-game locker room, I caught a moment between Frankie and the player who'd dropped the go-ahead pass. Frankie typed something. The kid read it silently, then nodded.

"What'd he say?" I asked later.

The kid looked at me and smiled. "He said, 'You dropped a pass. You didn't drop your team.'"

That stuck with him. Stuck with me, too.

As the field emptied and the stadium lights began to dim, I sat alone on a bench, replaying every snap, every play, every missed opportunity. The sharp sting of defeat pressed down on me; it was suffocating. What could we have done differently? Where did we fall short? The burden of what we hadn't achieved felt unbearable.

Out of the corner of my eye, I saw a shadow steadily approaching—a silhouette I knew well. It was Frankie, moving toward me with quiet resolve in the fading light. He positioned his chair directly in front of me, close enough that I couldn't look anywhere but at him.

He began to type. The rhythmic clicks of his clenched hand against the board broke the silence. Finally, the message appeared. "How are you doing?"

I looked at him, then shrugged. I didn't have words. The disappointment was too raw, the loss still fresh.

Frankie held my gaze, his hands moving again. He smiled faintly as the message formed. Just five words but they landed like a thunderclap.

"The only disability is a bad attitude."

I stared at the words, my frustration softening into something else. A smile tugged at the corners of my mouth. Frankie didn't need to say more. Here was a man who faced challenges far greater than anything I was grappling with—challenges most of us couldn't even imagine—and yet, there he sat, resolute and hopeful. In those simple words, Frankie had delivered a truth I needed to hear and the lesson I needed to learn.

I had spent the entire week preaching resilience, preaching perseverance, preaching Kipling's timeless message from "If"—that triumph and disaster are both impostors. But in the fog of disappointment, I had let the scoreboard cloud my vision. Frankie hadn't. He was living it. Frankie embodied it. His life, his example, was a reminder that our response to adversity is what defines us, not the outcome.

As I sat there, humbled and inspired, the loss no longer felt as devastating. Frankie had once again brought me back to center. The scoreboard didn't tell the whole story. It never does. What mattered was how we fought, how we believed in one another, and how we carried ourselves in both victory and defeat.

With renewed clarity, I stood up. Frankie nodded slightly, his smile lingering. He didn't need to say it, but I knew: It was time to move forward.

In that moment, his simple reminder, "the only disability is a bad attitude," reignited my perspective. Frankie had a way of cutting through noise and self-pity with undeniable clarity.

"Ready to get back to work?" he typed next. "We have a game next week."

And just like that, the haze lifted. Frankie was right. This wasn't the end; it was just one chapter in a much larger story. The loss didn't define us, but our response to it would.

As I stood and walked with Frankie off the field, the stadium lights dimming behind us, I realized that his quiet determination had taught me one of the most profound lessons of my life: Attitude is everything. It's not about avoiding failure or hardship; it's about how we choose to meet them. It's about showing up with grace when it's hard, with grit when it hurts, and with a quiet certainty that we can rise again, no matter how far we've fallen.

Life doesn't hand out guarantees. No matter how carefully we plan or how hard we work, there will be moments that shake us. Moments that don't go our way. But it's in those moments—not the easy ones—when our true character is revealed.

That's what Frankie taught me. The only disability is a bad attitude. He didn't just say it, he lived it. And resilient leaders? They meet adversity with presence, with perspective, and with purpose.

Greatness isn't about being the strongest or the most gifted. It belongs to those who refuse to be defined by the moment they're in.

A positive attitude isn't just an equalizer, it's a force. A mindset that frees us from excuses and unlocks what's possible.

Own it, and no setback is final. No dream out of reach.

POWERFUL WAYS TO MAKE ATTITUDE YOUR GREATEST ADVANTAGE

CHOOSE POSITIVITY DAILY

Your attitude starts with a choice. Begin each day by focusing on the positive aspects of life through gratitude, affirmations, or simply looking for the good in people and situations.

CULTIVATE SELF-BELIEF

Confidence fuels a strong attitude. Regularly affirm your strengths and past successes to remind yourself that you can handle whatever comes your way.

FOCUS ON SOLUTIONS, NOT PROBLEMS

Instead of dwelling on obstacles, shift your energy toward solutions. A solution-oriented mindset turns setbacks into actionable steps forward.

PRACTICE GRATITUDE, EVEN IN DIFFICULT TIMES

Gratitude alters your perspective. By focusing on what you're thankful for, even during challenges, you train your mind to remain optimistic and resilient.

TAKE OWNERSHIP OF YOUR REACTIONS

Your attitude is shaped by how you respond, not by the events themselves. Practice emotional intelligence by owning your reactions and maintaining control over your mindset.

By focusing on these principles, you can turn your attitude into a powerful advantage that helps you face challenges, build resilience, and thrive.

IN THE WORDS OF THOSE WHO LIVED IT

I've played football at the highest levels in college, and now I'm fortunate to be playing in the NFL. This isn't meant to downplay the incredible coaches I've worked with along the way, but more to highlight the impact of Coach Malleo: He's the best coach I've ever had. His ability to see the game—and life—differently than anyone else I've encountered set him apart. If he said something was going to happen, it happened.

Coach Malleo told me I was going to play in the NFL long before I even had serious college interest. At the time, I didn't believe it. But his conviction was absolute, and eventually, his belief in me became my own. Now, here I am, living the dream he saw in me before I could see it in myself.

If Coach Malleo was Batman, then Coach Kineavy was his Robin. They worked seamlessly together, always having each other's backs. It was obvious to all of us how much they cared—not just for the game but for each other and for us. Their leadership wasn't just about football; it was about building relationships and pushing us to be the very best versions of ourselves.

Playing football at Peddie was one of the best times of my life, and I owe so much of where I am today to that coaching staff. Coach Kineavy inspired me to strive for more, to be better every day. And Coach Malleo? He simply wouldn't let me be anything less than my best.

SirVocea Dennis
LB/ATH/Captain, Peddie Football (2018)
LB, University of Pittsburgh Football, '22 (Third Team All American)
2023, Fifth Round Draft Pick, Tampa Bay Buccaneers

LESSON 4

Growth Begins Where Comfort Ends

> It takes courage…to endure the sharp pains of self-discovery rather than choose
> to take the dull pain of unconsciousness that would last the rest of our lives.
> —MARIANNE WILLIAMSON

IT WAS AN UNSEASONABLY WARM WINTER DAY IN 2009, even by Arizona
standards. I had moved there to train for professional football—chasing
a dream I'd nurtured since childhood. My days were consumed with
workouts designed to break you down and build you back stronger.
That afternoon's session had done exactly that.

My shirt clung to me, soaked through with sweat, as I peeled it off
and climbed into my car. The sun-scorched leather burned against
my skin. I cranked the A/C to full blast, letting the cool air wash
over me in short, rhythmic bursts. My lungs ached. My legs shook.
But the discomfort felt earned.

The dashboard thermometer blinked ninety degrees—a cruel reminder that even winter bowed to the desert heat. I leaned the seat
back to catch my breath. And then my phone buzzed.

It was my father.

"Chris," he said, his voice heavy, "It's your mom." I sat upright,
gripping the steering wheel with one hand and the phone with the
other. "She's been diagnosed with cancer," he continued, the words

cutting through the whistle of the air conditioning. "Pancreatic. Stage 4."

For a moment, everything went silent. The air in the car seemed to thicken, pressing down on my chest. The phrase *Stage 4* echoed in my mind, each repetition sharper than the last.

"Stage 4?" I repeated, my voice breaking, as if saying it out loud might make it less real.

I reached for my water bottle, desperate to find something to anchor myself. I took a sip, but the water tasted sour, like it had been tainted by the news I'd just heard. My stomach churned as I set the bottle back down.

My mother—my vibrant, fun-loving, endlessly optimistic mother—was dying. The woman who could fill any room with laughter, who had a knack for turning the mundane into something magical, was now fighting a battle against a formidable opponent.

I stared out the windshield, my vision blurring as tears welled up. Outside, life went on with cruel indifference. A car pulled into a nearby space, while a man emerged from the gym laughing into his phone. The normalcy was deafening against the quiet chaos inside me.

After moving to Arizona to train for professional football, I had gone home for the holidays and noticed my mom wasn't quite herself. She seemed more fatigued, her energy dimmed. It was so subtle that I didn't think much of it at the time.

To say I was shocked to hear she had cancer is an understatement. My mom was the epitome of health and vitality. She had never smoked or drank, ate a clean diet, and moved through life with purpose. As a swim instructor and high school English teacher, she was always active, always giving, and always full of life.

Now, living nearly twenty-five hundred miles away, I felt helpless. An unbearable weight descended in the face of such devastating news.

But helplessness wasn't an option for our family. With the support of loved ones, we circled the wagons and went on the attack. We sought out alternative medical treatments, refusing to accept the limitations of conventional timelines. We shielded my mom from the grim predictions doctors often imposed. They couldn't measure love or the resilience of the human spirit, and we clung to that belief as if our lives depended on it. In many ways, they did.

We made the decision to move my mom to Arizona for treatment. I got a front-row seat to her fight. It was brutal, beautiful, and something I'll carry with me forever. My mom faced her illness with a combination of grace and ferocity. She became fearless, gritty, and steadfast in her resolve. Each doctor's appointment that brought good news—a shrinking tumor or a stable scan—became a cause for celebration. Her strength was awe-inspiring. She was getting better. Until one day, she wasn't.

Now, as her body began to fail, I sat on the edge of the hospice bed, surrounded by the soft beeping of medical machines and the faint scent of lavender lotion—her favorite, the one we always used to keep her hands soft. The shades were drawn, allowing just a sliver of late afternoon light to filter in, casting a warm glow on the room's pale, neutral walls. Framed family photos rested on the side table with our smiles frozen in happier times.

That room—her final resting place—felt impossibly small for a woman whose presence had filled every corner of my life.

She was my rock, my constant, my everything. The woman who always greeted me with open arms after a long practice. The one who made me feel like I could conquer the world with her steadfast faith in me. Now, her body had grown frail, but her spirit, as always, remained composed.

She turned to me, her voice soft but steady, delivering the words with the poise and courage only she possessed. "My mind and heart are strong and fighting, but my body is failing me."

Hearing those words pierced me like nothing else ever had. I gripped her hand tightly, as if holding onto her could keep the inevitable at bay. But I knew. Her battle had been long and valiant, but she was slipping away.

I sat in silence, unable to move. The world hadn't changed—but mine had collapsed.

Soon after that, she was gone.

For anyone who has ever lost a parent, you know the void it leaves; a space in your heart that no amount of time or healing can ever fill. But her words stayed with me, "My mind and heart are strong and fighting, but my body is failing me."

Those words became a rallying cry for me, a reminder that when life feels insurmountable and the body falters, our spirit and resolve can carry us through. Her voice lives on within me, urging me forward when the weight of life feels too much to bear.

It's a tragedy that so many people face the opposite crisis. Their bodies are strong, yet they allow negativity to seep into their hearts and minds, eroding their strength from within. The quiet toll of self-doubt, toxic relationships, and a life devoid of purpose is often unseen but deeply destructive. It strips us of our resilience, our joy, and our belief in what's possible, until all that remains is a shadow of who we could have been.

In the end, no matter how strong or healthy we are, our bodies will inevitably break down. That's the nature of life. But our hearts and minds can rise and endure if we choose to nurture them. To honor my mother's strength, I resolved to cultivate an unbeatable heart and mind and to inspire others to do the same.

It wasn't until years later, when I met Frankie, that I recognized the same resilient spirit I saw in my mom alive in someone else. I saw someone who embodied what it meant to have the heart and mind of a warrior, even when the body refused to cooperate—a resolve that couldn't be measured by physical ability alone.

The truth about Frankie's life is that the extreme form of cerebral palsy he lives with is unforgiving and often tremendously painful. Every single basic need must be attended to. His body betrays him with spasms, and his hands clench tightly, making it a struggle to type even a single word on his communication board. Velcro straps secure his legs to keep them from kicking involuntarily, and his wheelchair—heavy and cumbersome—turns even the simplest terrain into a challenge. A freshly paved parking lot becomes an obstacle; the uneven ground of a football field can feel impossible to navigate.

And yet, Frankie hardly falters. He meets most challenges with quiet defiance and an unbeatable spirit, reminding everyone around him that strength is not found in ease—it's forged in the struggle. His resilience isn't just inspiring, it's life changing for those who witness it. It forces you to ask yourself: *What's holding me back?* Because when you see someone with every reason to give up choosing instead to rise, you can't help but reevaluate your own excuses.

What struck me most, however, was the change I witnessed in Frankie himself over those four years we worked together. It wasn't just the team that grew stronger—it was him. Frankie made a deliberate and courageous choice to step into an unfamiliar world, a world brimming with obstacles he couldn't fully predict. The road ahead was anything but smooth, and the terrain—both literal and metaphorical—was rocky and unkind. Yet, he embraced it without hesitation.

Frankie understood something that many of us spend our entire lives trying to grasp: Pain, discomfort, and effort are not barriers, they're the building blocks of growth. He leaned into the hard moments, knowing they would shape him into someone even stronger, someone capable of an impact far beyond what he might have imagined. By showing up every day, by refusing to let his challenges define him, Frankie reminded us all that greatness isn't born from comfort. It's forged in the courage to keep moving forward, no matter how difficult the journey.

When Frankie first joined our coaching staff, he was already equipped with intelligence, creativity, passion, and talent. But what he lacked was the self-belief to rise to his highest potential. He couldn't yet see in himself what I and others so clearly saw—a strength and capability that were waiting to be unleashed.

With every task he embraced and challenge he confronted, Frankie chipped away at the layers of discomfort and self-doubt. Each roll forward, no matter how small, built his confidence. Slowly but surely, Frankie evolved into someone who no longer hesitated or shrank from the spotlight. He stood tall, undaunted, self-assured, and fully aware that his presence and contributions weren't just valuable; they were profoundly impactful.

Not long after he joined our staff, Frankie became a beloved fixture on campus. Most people simply called him Coach K, a title he wore with pride as he wheeled from place to place, spreading joy and proper perspective to everyone he encountered. His laugh was infectious, his insight sharp, and his presence a constant reminder of the resilience and purpose we all aspired to embody.

One morning, I was sitting in my office in the admissions building, reflecting on the day ahead. The space had recently been renovated, and the smell of fresh paint and new carpet lingered in the air, mingling with the faint scent of coffee wafting in from an adjacent office. The morning light poured through the large window behind me, bathing the room in a warm glow and offering a glimpse of the campus waking up to another day.

I'd arranged the office to feel open and inviting. My desk was positioned against the side wall, leaving nothing between me and anyone who came to visit. I'd always disliked the formality of a desk as a barrier; I wanted guests to feel like they could sit down and speak freely. Above the desk hung a large, framed sign that read, "I eat grit for breakfast"—a gift from a thoughtful colleague who knew how much I loved idioms and what they could inspire.

I had set up the office with Frankie in mind. I knew he would become a regular visitor, and I wanted to make it as easy as possible for him to wheel in and out. Frankie thrived on connection, and I wanted him to feel like this space was just as much his as it was mine.

Near the opposite wall sat two plush blue leather chairs, angled slightly toward each other, their deep colors mirroring those of our school. They weren't just furniture—they were witnesses to countless moments of raw emotion.

If chairs could talk, these two would have stories to tell. They had supported young men as they cried tears of frustration when life dealt them blows they didn't know how to handle. They had cradled players as they laughed with relief and joy when a college extended a scholarship offer that would change their lives.

Those chairs weren't just the eight legs of comfort—they were pillars of trust, absorbing the weight of every triumph, every failure, and every dream shared within the walls of that office.

Frankie rolled in, energy radiating through every pore as if his very presence could light up the room. I looked up from the paperwork in front of me, immediately turning my attention to him. He motioned for me, and by this point in our relationship, I didn't need words to know that whatever he was about to share was big.

"They are asking me to speak," he typed, his eyes alight with nervous energy.

"Speak where?" I said, tilting my head with curiosity.

"C-H-A-P-E-L," he replied, spelling it out slowly.

He didn't need to say anything more. I knew exactly what he meant.

"They want YOU to speak at chapel?" My mind began to race.

Ayer Memorial Chapel was dedicated in 1951 to honor the young Peddie men who had died in World War II. It was one of the most iconic buildings on Peddie's campus. Stately and timeless, it was constructed from red brick and topped with a white steeple that seemed to stretch toward the heavens, basking in the light by day and standing steadfast under the glow of the moon and stars by night.

Twice a week, the entire Peddie community—students, faculty, dining hall staff—gathered in that sacred space to reflect on the school's values and hear from speakers who embodied those values. That podium had held presidents, governors, scientists, scholars, and even a young Dr. Martin Luther King Jr.

Now, Frankie was being asked to take his place on that storied stage, addressing over five hundred members of the Peddie community.

I leaned back in my office chair, overwhelmed by the significance of Frankie's news. My thoughts began to spiral back to our first interview, to the questions that had once seemed so natural but now felt limiting. *Why didn't anyone tell me about this? How are you going to speak for twenty minutes? Who is going to help you? When is this supposed to happen? You have to decline, right?*

But I stopped myself before the questions could spill out. This wasn't about doubts or logistics. This was about Frankie.

The school chaplain, Marc, a seasoned man with a rough exterior but a heart of gold, had extended the invitation. Chaplain Marc was the kind of person who could navigate the complexities of a tough New York City bar as effortlessly as he commanded respect at the pulpit. His gruff voice and straightforward demeanor masked a deep well of empathy and wisdom.

Chaplain Marc had seen Frankie wheeling through campus, bringing his unique energy and perspective to every interaction. Over time, he'd gotten to know him, heard his story, and had watched the quiet but profound impact Frankie had on those around him.

He felt the community needed to know Frankie the way he had come to know him—not just as a coach or a figure on campus, but as a man with a powerful story and a message worth sharing. Chaplain Marc saw Frankie as someone who could challenge the school to reflect, grow, and embrace the deeper values that defined the Peddie spirit.

And so, confident Frankie would rise to the occasion, Chaplain Marc extended the invitation. By speaking at chapel, Frankie would connect with the soul of the community in a way few others could.

I doubt Frankie would have agreed to speak when he first joined our coaching staff. Back then, he was still finding his footing—or, rather, his wheels—within the program. He observed quietly, contributed thoughtfully, and let his presence speak louder than his voice.

But over time, Frankie embraced the opportunity to grow. He took on new challenges with determination, peeling away the layers of insecurity and stepping boldly into his greatness. He had transitioned from a quiet observer to an integral voice on campus—someone who inspired not only through his actions but now through his words.

"What do you think?" I asked him. "Do you want to do it?"

"Yes," he replied without hesitation, pausing before adding, "But only if you will introduce me."

His response was confident but carried a faint vulnerability, as if he were stepping onto unfamiliar ground. I could feel my own nerves swell. I was anxious for him and could only imagine the emotions swirling within him.

But Frankie knew what needed to be done. He understood that growth doesn't come from comfort, and this was his moment to lead by example. By standing in front of our community, he would show them—show all of us—what it meant to embrace discomfort in the name of growth.

The morning of Frankie's address, I arrived early to prepare for my introduction, hoping to balance my thoughts.

As I walked up the iconic steps of Ayer Memorial Chapel, I paused, staring at the towering white steeple. Its grandeur felt almost symbolic of the day ahead. Pulling open the doors, I was greeted by the scent of aged wood and faint mustiness—an old church full of stories and history.

Inside the lobby, memorial plaques lined the walls, honoring the young men for whom the chapel had been dedicated. Their names, etched into bronze, were a solemn reminder of legacy, sacrifice, and the weight of this sacred space.

I made my way down the long central aisle, each step creaking beneath me, the sound amplified in the empty, cavernous sanctuary. The chandeliers overhead were illuminated by the morning light filtering through the windows and casting shadows on the wooden pews.

As I approached the pulpit, I noticed the freshly vacuumed lines woven into the red-patterned carpet beneath my feet, each one a meticulous detail preparing for the day's event.

Standing at the pulpit, I ran my hand along its smooth edge, imagining the important voices that had stood here before. And now it would hold Frankie's message, a message that carried with it a large measure of perseverance and courage.

Slowly, the chapel began to fill with teenagers and faculty. Word had spread across campus that Frankie would be speaking, and everyone wanted a seat. The air buzzed with excitement and curiosity.

The pews filled quickly, students crammed shoulder to shoulder, their whispered conversations echoing off the high ceilings. Faculty members lined the outer aisles, their backs pressed against the walls, as if wanting to both observe and leave room for the spotlight Frankie deserved.

The energy in the room shifted as Frankie entered from the side of the chapel, accompanied by two student volunteers who carefully guided his chair down the center aisle. His presence was magnetic—each turn of his wheels seemed to command attention without demanding it. As he reached the front, he gave a nod to the tech team stationed beside the pulpit. They adjusted the microphone height and double-checked the voice box, while Frankie settled into position below the towering lectern, exactly where he wanted to be—not elevated above the crowd, but among it.

From the back of the chapel, students craned their necks hoping for a glimpse of the special speaker. Microphones had been meticulously placed to ensure every word would carry to the farthest reaches of the room. His speech, carefully prerecorded to account for his physical challenges, would play through the voice box, delivering his message with clarity and precision.

I stepped to the microphone at the pulpit looking down on the crowd and Frankie, the importance of the moment almost crushing me as I faced the school community. Hundreds of eyes stared back, while my own gaze was fixed on the back of Frankie's head, his determination radiating even to where I stood.

After a deep breath, I addressed the crowd, introducing Frankie and his story with as much care and respect as I could muster.

"There are people who speak to our minds, and there are people who speak to our hearts. Frankie is one of the rare few who does both without ever needing to raise his voice. Today, you won't just hear his story, you'll feel the strength behind it."

The words came easily as if they had been patiently waiting for that moment. Finally, I stepped off the podium and found my seat on a nearby pew. The unforgiving wood dug into my legs and back as I sat down, rigid with anticipation. I closed my eyes and whispered a simple prayer: *Please let this go well.*

The room was silent. Frankie leaned forward slightly and pressed play on his recorder.

"Hello, everyone. My name is Frankie Kineavy," the voice began—metallic and mechanical, sounding more like a robot at a drive-through speaker than a person. For a split second, my stomach dropped.

But then something remarkable happened.

Frankie's words began to flow, and as he spoke of perseverance, grit, and the challenges he had faced, the voice—though synthesized—softened, gained rhythm, and deepened. The warmth of Frankie's message and the truth he laid bare for all to hear filled the room, and suddenly, it wasn't just a machine speaking. It was Frankie.

"I've never yelled to get someone's attention. I've never run a race or climbed a mountain. But I've learned how to be patient. How to listen. How to keep showing up when people doubt you. And sometimes, that's its own kind of victory."

A hush settled over the chapel. You could feel the air shift. Every head was lifted, every eye locked in.

The machine was speaking. But it was Frankie we heard.

I opened my eyes and looked out at the crowd. Jaws hung open in disbelief. Students who moments ago had been whispering to one another now sat utterly captivated. Faculty wiped at tear-filled eyes with tissues pulled hastily from pockets. Hearts swelled with every word, Frankie's message settling into the collective soul of the room.

The machine was speaking. But it was Frankie we heard.

As the final words of his speech trailed off, there was a heartbeat of silence. No one moved. Then one clap, sharp and defiant, rang out from the back.

It began with a single senior, rising to his feet, another stood, and then another, and before I knew it, the entire room was on its feet. The sound was deafening—a celebration unlike anything this chapel had ever seen.

I sat there, almost in disbelief, watching the community rise in unison for Frankie. He had done it. He had taken the stage—his stage—and delivered a message that moved an entire room to its feet.

I looked around and knew this room would never forget today.

What if I had let my own limiting beliefs stand in his way? What if I had doubted his ability and said no? What if Frankie hadn't had the courage to say yes? None of us would have experienced the beauty of what had just unfolded.

Frankie's willingness to step into the unknown, to push beyond his comfort zone, wasn't just an act of bravery—it was a gift. A gift that reminded us all that the most powerful moments in life come when we dare to believe in ourselves and each other, even when doubt whispers otherwise.

Growth demands pain and discomfort; there's no shortcut around it. The journey is rarely easy, but it's always worth it. And here's the truth: The "perfect" moment we so often wait for never comes. Growth doesn't happen when we feel ready, it happens when we take action despite feeling unprepared. If you want to grow, to pursue the life you dream of, you must start where you are, with what you have, right now. Because time won't wait, and neither will the moment that could change everything.

Avoiding discomfort is easy. It's human nature to gravitate toward what's safe and predictable. But life and leadership demand more. They require the courage to step into the fire; not for personal glory, but to clear a path for others.

Leaders who avoid discomfort or refuse to confront their weaknesses may preserve the status quo, but they'll never create lasting impact. That's how institutions falter, businesses crumble, and relationships break down—by clinging to the fleeting security of comfort.

In both Frankie and my mom, I witnessed firsthand what growth can do to the human spirit. They faced challenges that would break most people. Yet they rose, each in their own way, with courage and grace.

My mom, in the final months of her life, showed me what it means to fight with everything you have, even when the odds are stacked against you. Her body may have been failing, but her heart and mind stayed resilient.

Frankie, too, lived a daily battle with physical limitations. But inch by inch, he chose to embrace the struggle. He kept showing up, kept saying yes to new challenges and refusing to let his circumstances define him.

So let this be your call to action: Be like them.

Choose growth—even when it's hard.

Push forward—even when it feels impossible.

Step into the challenge.

Embrace the discomfort.

Strengthen your heart. Sharpen your mind. Let your spirit fight like hell.

Because it's in those moments of struggle, when everything inside us wants to quit, that we uncover who we truly are.

POWERFUL WAYS TO GROW THROUGH CHALLENGE

EMBRACE DISCOMFORT AS A TEACHER

Actively seek situations that challenge your comfort zones. Take on a project, task, or role that intimidates you or forces you to develop new skills. Reflect on moments of discomfort in your past and identify the growth they produced. Use these insights to reframe future challenges as opportunities for growth.

CULTIVATE RESILIENCE THROUGH SMALL WINS

Break large, intimidating goals into smaller, manageable tasks. Celebrate each small victory as evidence of your progress and capability.

DEVELOP A STRONG FOUNDATION

Focus on consistent, unseen work that builds your character, knowledge, and skills. Dedicate time to daily practices such as journaling, learning, or physical training. Understand that growth often happens below the surface. Be patient and trust the process even when immediate results aren't visible.

COMMIT TO LIFELONG GROWTH

Regularly evaluate areas of your life where comfort may be holding you back. Commit to continuous improvement, whether in relationships, career, or personal growth. Create a growth mindset by embracing feedback, learning from failures, and seeking mentorship to challenge your perspectives.

These steps will help you foster growth and leadership that leave a lasting impact.

IN THE WORDS OF THOSE WHO LIVED IT

Coach Malleo and Coach Kineavy, along with the entire Peddie football program, did not just train me in football—they helped me forge my will and create a disposition that not just welcomed adversity, but was comfortable in it. My time at Peddie was not easy, but value does not come from easy. I'm grateful to have been a part of the program. Coach Kineavy, despite immense challenges, displayed incredible resilience, and no one, especially Coach Malleo, expected less of him. He was as much a part of the team and the coaching staff as anyone else. That's a testament to the culture of embracing adversity that Coach Malleo created and was the foundation of the Peddie football program. It was an amazing place.

Elic Ayomanor
WR, Peddie Football (2019)
WR, Stanford University Football, '24 (First Team Freshman All American '23)
2025, Fourth Round Pick Tennessee Titans

LESSON 5

Enjoy the Journey

It's not the mountain we conquer, but ourselves.

—SIR EDMUND HILLARY

THE LOCKER ROOM WAS QUIET—so quiet I could hear my heartbeat in the stillness.

I was the first one in. I sat on the blue folding chair in front of my locker, the leather cold against my legs. A small chip in the wood framing the locker caught my eye. Someone must've thrown a helmet.

Above me, a silver nameplate—Chris Malleo—rested above a red NFL practice jersey. Number 11. Freshly pressed. Centered like it belonged. I reached out and ran my fingers across the mesh. It felt rough. Familiar. Unreal. I had made it. Somehow, I was here.

And suddenly, everything came rushing back: Five a.m. lifts in silent weight rooms lit by flickering fluorescents. Two-hour drives from practice to my mom's chemo treatments. Long bus rides through nameless towns, staring out windows into nothing, daring to believe this dream wasn't a lie. Practices where I was overlooked. Film rooms where I studied plays I'd never get to run.

No headlines. No glory. Just grit.

I never got my shot at quarterback in college. But I trained like I had one. And somehow, it worked. The Toronto Argonauts in the Canadian Football League signed me. Then an indoor team in Reading, Pennsylvania. Then this: tryouts for the New York Giants.

I grabbed the helmet, took a deep breath, and for a second, I was eight years old again in our backyard in New Jersey, plastic helmet wobbling on my head, grass stains on my jeans.

But this wasn't pretend. This was my shot.

I stood slowly, cradling the helmet in my hands. The silence clung to me as I walked down the tunnel, each step echoing off the walls. Then, sunlight. Shouts. The sudden blast of energy that only the field could bring. The world shifted from stillness to speed, and there was no turning back.

The sharp sound of a whistle snapped me out of it.

The urgency of the field took over—cleats pounding, coaches barking, bodies moving in sync. Suddenly the ball was in my hands. My feet dropped back, my grip found the laces, and the world fell away.

Spiral after spiral left my hand, crisp and clean. Every throw felt effortless—a lifetime of preparation channeled into minutes. My body was a machine. My mind was quiet.

The tryout ended. They told us to shower and meet in the team room. I lingered, walking off the field slowly. Sweat ran down my face. My legs ached. But my spirit? It felt light.

I could do this forever, I thought.

We gathered in the team room. A coach stepped up and thanked us for coming. His voice was flat. Procedural. Then he began reading names.

I waited.

But mine wasn't called.

I sat there, frozen. The voices, the scrape of chairs, the polite shuffling—it all blurred into background noise. They hadn't called my name.

I was the only quarterback there. I had performed. I had delivered. I had done everything right.

Still, nothing.

Eventually, I stood. My legs felt heavy. As I turned toward the door, a hand caught my arm. It was the quarterbacks' coach. His eyes said everything before his mouth opened. "It wasn't because you weren't good enough," he said quietly.

I swallowed. "Then what was it?"

He paused. "Sometimes the numbers don't work in your favor."

That was it. Not my play. Not my effort. Just the numbers. Somehow, that hurt more than anything.

I left without another word. Out the building. Through the lot. Into my car. Slammed the door.

Silence.

Then rage.

I punched the steering wheel again and again until my hand throbbed. Until it felt real. Until the ache in my chest had somewhere to land.

My hand pulsed. My heart ached. And all I could think about was telling my mom. This wasn't how the story was supposed to end.

I had pictured her watching me from a hospital bed, smiling. I thought if I made it, she might keep fighting. Maybe she'd hold on longer. Maybe I could give her that. But now? Now all I had was the silence.

It was an unfair pressure to put on myself. I see that now. But back then, I wasn't thinking clearly. I had been consumed by the outcome. Every throw, every step, every sacrifice—I thought it was all leading to this. And when it didn't happen, I felt hollow. I didn't ask myself how far I'd come. I only saw the distance left.

But here's what I've learned since then: I should have been proud. Not because I made it, but because I kept going. The sacrifices, the risks, the criticism, the doubt—I faced it all and didn't flinch. That's success. Not being seen. Not being chosen. But becoming someone who refuses to quit.

That was the gift. And I didn't even know I had it yet.

It wasn't until years later, when I met Frankie, that I finally understood: The journey is far more important than the destination.

When I first met Frankie, his physical limitations were impossible to ignore. But what struck me most wasn't what he couldn't do—it was what he *wouldn't stop doing.* He never allowed circumstances to define him.

Frankie didn't measure success by outcomes. He measured it by how hard he worked, and he always gave everything he had.

Our Peddie practice field became the perfect backdrop for this mindset. It was a place where effort was celebrated as much as achievement. Tucked at the edge of campus, the field was more than just a space for drills and plays; it was a testing ground for perseverance and growth. To reach it, players had to traverse a gravel path that sloped down before sharply rising again—a fitting metaphor for the challenges life inevitably throws our way. For Frankie, however, the journey to the field was steeper in every sense.

With the help of his aide, Frankie was typically driven to the field's edge in a special van. Once there, he relied on a machine to carefully exit the vehicle, his wheelchair rolling steadily onto the uneven ground. From drill to drill, he moved with quiet determination, making observations he would share with me during practice or in the moments that followed.

One afternoon, the sky dimmed, and a quiet wind swept across the practice field, hinting at

> But what struck me most wasn't what he couldn't do—it was what he wouldn't stop doing.

a storm. As practice began, Frankie's van was nowhere to be seen. I assumed he might be running late, but as the minutes ticked by and the van still didn't appear, I began to feel uneasy. Frankie was one of the most dependable people I'd ever met. He never missed practice without letting me know. This tardiness was unlike him, and it gnawed at me.

By mid-practice, my concern got the better of me. I texted Frankie's aide to check in. The reply I received made my heart sink: Frankie had a substitute aide that day, and unfamiliar with the routine, they had dropped him off at the far end of the road, assuming he could manage the rest on his own.

I looked toward the path. The sky was dark now. Something was wrong. Frankie was out there—alone—facing a climb that challenged even our strongest players. My chest tightened.

I assigned an assistant coach to oversee practice and took off running toward the gravel road. The sky split open and the rain hit like it was trying to wash the gravel away. The rain came fast—thick sheets slamming the gravel, blurring the road ahead. My shoes slipped. My lungs burned. But I didn't stop.

In the distance, I spotted him. His chair rocked back and forth in place, stuck in the loose gravel. The wheels spun but didn't catch. He was soaked, arms moving, still trying. Relief and heartbreak hit me at the same time.

When I finally reached him, I dropped to my knees in the mud beside the chair. Rain dripped from the brim of my hat. My breath came fast.

"Are you okay?" I asked, my voice low. Careful. Expecting frustration, maybe even defeat.

Frankie looked up at me, drenched, breathless, unmoved by the chaos around him. He typed, then waited. "Did you see how far I made it?"

His words stopped me in my tracks. Even now, as I write this, I get choked up thinking about that moment.

Years earlier, as I sat alone in the parking lot of an NFL facility pounding the steering wheel in frustration and shame, my focus was on what I hadn't achieved. What I didn't have. I let the disappointment consume me—blind to the road I'd taken just to get there.

And here was Frankie—sopping wet, spent, and beaming with pride—celebrating twenty yards of hard-earned progress like he'd crossed a marathon finish line.

That day, Frankie gave me a masterclass in perspective. Where I had once seen failure, he saw victory. His pride wasn't tied to the distance—only to the effort. He could've stopped. The rain, the gravel, and the hill all said he should. But he didn't. He kept going. Inch by inch.

That was the moment everything shifted in my mind and heart. As a coach, I started to see my job differently. It wasn't about pushing players toward a finish line. It was about helping them see their own progress. To celebrate the small wins. To honor the grind. To find pride in every rep, every sprint, every step forward—no matter how small.

And when they did? Something lit up in them. Belief. Hunger. Grit. It changed our team.

We still chased wins, but we celebrated the effort that got us there. And as that culture grew, so did their confidence. Their resilience. Their trust in the process. Because when people can see how far they've come, they begin to believe in how far they can go.

> Because when people can see how far they've come, they begin to believe in how far they can go.

So let me ask you: What are the twenty yards you're fighting for today? What progress are you overlooking just because it doesn't seem like a win yet?

Show up anyway.

Keep pushing.

Inch by inch.

Because one day you'll look back, not at the finish line, but at the stretch of gravel behind you, and say, "Look how far I made it."

POWERFUL WAYS TO ENJOY THE JOURNEY

PAUSE AND REFLECT

Take a moment to acknowledge your progress and how it contributes to your larger goals. Reflection helps reinforce the significance of your effort and boosts your sense of accomplishment.

KEEP A SUCCESS JOURNAL

Document your small victories and how they made you feel. Revisiting these entries can remind you of how far you've come and inspire you during challenging times.

CREATE A VISUAL REMINDER

Use a progress board, vision board, or "victory wall" to visually track your achievements. Seeing your milestones displayed can keep you motivated and provide a tangible reminder of your growth.

BUILD ON MOMENTUM

Use each small victory as a stepping stone toward your next goal. Set new mini-goals that build on your progress, ensuring you stay motivated and continuously moving forward.

By celebrating your small victories, you build a habit of acknowledging progress, reinforcing positive behavior, and keeping yourself motivated for the bigger challenges ahead. These celebrations help create a mindset where success is seen as a journey, not just a destination.

IN THE WORDS OF THOSE WHO LIVED IT

I had the privilege of coaching alongside Coach Malleo and Coach Kineavy, giving me a front-row seat to witness the tremendous men and leaders they are. I consider myself incredibly fortunate to have been part of this program and to have seen firsthand the amazing leader that Coach Malleo is. When we hired Coach Kineavy, everything Coach Malleo was working to create reached an entirely new level. The culture they built together was nothing short of extraordinary.

At the time, I was entrusted with coaching the wide receivers, even though I wasn't old enough to legally have a drink. Imagine being twenty years old and having these incredible men as your mentors. They taught me lessons not only about football but also about life, leadership, and what it means to strive for excellence. The culture they cultivated wasn't something you'd expect to find in high school football—it was truly remarkable.

Under their guidance, I witnessed a program that embodied discipline, hard work, and respect. Their passion and dedication made Peddie football a family, and being part of it felt like being part of something greater than ourselves. To this day, I cherish the memories and the people who made them so special.

The world is lucky to have access to the stories and lessons of Coach Malleo and Coach Kineavy. Their leadership doesn't just change teams—it transforms lives. I am a better person for having known them, and I know their impact will continue to inspire countless others.

Josh Holsopple
WRs Coach
Peddie Football (2014–2019)

LESSON 6

Have a Bold Vision

> It always seems impossible until it is done.
>
> —NELSON MANDELA

ON THE EVENING BEFORE THANKSGIVING IN 2001, I stood on a hill as a high school junior, staring out at a frenzied sea of hometown fans gathered for our pep rally. The bonfire roared below, flames licking the night sky and sending sparks into the crisp fall air. Every cheer from the crowd seemed to amplify the fire's energy, and the atmosphere crackled with anticipation.

This wasn't just any rally. The next day, we would take the field against our biggest rival in a Thanksgiving Day showdown, reigniting a fierce rivalry that had lain dormant for eight long years. The buildup was unlike anything we had ever experienced. The weight of history, pride, and tradition hung in the air. Over twelve thousand fans were expected to fill the stands.

Our opponents came into the game riding an incredible thirty-four-game winning streak. They called it "The Streak." To them, it was a badge of honor. To us, it was an open challenge—one we couldn't wait to take on.

Both teams were well-coached, but their roster was undeniably more talented than ours. I could feel the nervous energy radiating from my teammates as we huddled together, their eyes darting toward the crowded stands. But for me, it felt different.

I felt ready.

For over a year, I had visualized this game. I pictured every moment in my head like a film on repeat—the walk onto the field, the deafening roar of the crowd, the sound of the whistle slicing through the cold air. I imagined how it would feel to stand there, not as someone overwhelmed by the stakes, but as someone prepared to meet the moment.

And now, standing before my teammates and the roaring crowd at this pep rally, I wasn't nervous. I was confident. I was calm. I was bold.

Fueled by that boldness—and maybe by a bit of teenage impulsiveness—I made my way to the microphone. The crowd quieted, their faces glowing in the flickering firelight as they waited to hear what I had to say.

I don't remember every word I spoke, but I remember how it felt. I spoke with conviction, my voice clear, building the crowd's energy with every line. The fire roared, the crowd leaned in, and I felt unstoppable.

Then, throwing caution—and probably a little common sense—to the wind, I delivered the line that would replay on local TV for the next twenty-four hours: "The Streak ends tomorrow. I guarantee victory!"

The crowd went wild. Cheers exploded into the night. My teammates roared, their nervous energy now replaced by adrenaline and belief. Somewhere in the chaos, I saw my head coach give me a look that was half proud and half panicked. If he could have tackled me to shut me up, I'm sure he would have (sorry, Coach Barnes). Across town, I can only imagine our rivals heard those words too. I doubt they found them nearly as entertaining.

The next morning, the stands were packed by sunrise. Cold air. High stakes. A wall of noise from the opening kickoff. Our rivals came out swinging. Fast. Physical. Every possession was a war. Still, we matched them hit for hit, drive for drive.

Then, in the second quarter, disaster struck. Our star running back, our best player, went down, clutching his leg. The crowd gasped. The sideline froze. You could feel the momentum shifting and belief beginning to slip. I turned to our backup, Mike Lackett, and locked eyes with him. "You're ready," I said. "You've been ready. Go take it."

At that moment, I wasn't speaking to just a backup—I was speaking to a close friend who stayed late, who never complained, who prepared for a spotlight he wasn't sure would come. But it came. And he was ready. No panic. No overthinking. Just confidence.

And then he ran wild.

Three touchdowns. All heart. All effort. He played like he had belonged there the whole time.

When the final whistle blew, the scoreboard read 20-6. We had done it.

I stood there for a second, just soaking it in—the cold air in my lungs, the weight of my helmet in my hand, the sound of disbelief turning into celebration all around me.

As I walked off the field, the world around me felt alive—like it was vibrating with joy. Fans poured out of the stands, their faces flushed with excitement, their voices hoarse from cheering. They grabbed me by the shoulders, pulling me into hugs that were equal parts laughter and disbelief. Hands tussled my hair as people shouted, "You called it! You called it!" Their words mixed with the roar of the crowd, but I could feel their pride in every embrace, every slap on the back.

I looked up and saw my teammates, some raising their helmets to the sky, others grinning ear to ear as they celebrated with family and friends. Parents were crying, students were cheering, and it felt like the entire town was there, wrapped up in this one shared victory.

As I kept walking, my cleats digging into the turf, I let it all hit me. I had spoken boldly, and we had delivered. In that moment—amid the hugs, the shouts, and the electric energy—I made a promise to myself: From that day forward, I would always hold onto bold visions, *so long as I was willing to back them up with bold actions*. Boldness, I realized, isn't recklessness. It's clarity. It's confidence. It's the willingness to act when others might hesitate.

I didn't just believe we could win, I knew it. That belief is what turns bold visions into extraordinary realities. It's the difference between dreaming about what's possible and stepping forward to make it so.

In my life, no one embodies boldness more profoundly than Frankie. The clarity and conviction in his vision for what he wants to achieve are nothing short of electrifying. Just hearing him speak about his dreams makes you want to leap out of your chair, find the nearest mountain, and start climbing.

All his life, people have tried to place cages around Frankie and his aspirations. They've underestimated him, defined him by his physical limitations, and attempted to narrow the scope of what he could accomplish. But Frankie refuses to let those limitations define him.

He is so deeply rooted in who he is and what he envisions for his life that no challenge, no judgment, and no obstacle can shake his resolve. His dreams are not just bold—they're boundless.

A key to life is surpassing your own expectations, and this includes not living down to the expectations of others. No one else can fully understand your makeup, your heart, your spirit, or your drive. The expectations others place on you should hold no weight because, more often than not, they'll underestimate what you're capable of.

Don't wait for someone else to raise the bar. Set it yourself and then chase it like your life depends on it. Because in a way, it does.

Frankie is the perfect embodiment of this truth. The boldness it took for him to email me, expressing his desire to join our staff, speaks volumes about his character and determination. Here was a man with significant physical limitations and no prior football coaching experience, yet he reached out with absolute conviction.

He didn't focus on the reasons he shouldn't take that step—the doubts, the perceived limitations, or the whispers of fear that would have stopped most people. Instead, he let his bold vision lead the way, driven by a purpose he refused to ignore.

Frankie's courage reminds us of something essential: When we align our actions with our purpose the barriers in front of us don't disappear, they reconstruct our resolve. What once seemed like obstacles become stepping stones to something greater.

Reflecting on Frankie's example brought clarity to my own life. It made me confront the fleeting nature of time and the urgent importance of living boldly.

Recently, my wife threw me a surprise birthday party. I was surrounded by friends, laughter, and thoughtful gifts that I'll always treasure. But one gift stood apart. My close friends Gary and Hope Stevenson flew in from Arizona to surprise me, carrying something that hit me like a punch to the chest: a framed calendar titled *Your Life in Weeks.*

It wasn't just a calendar, it was a roadmap of my life, reduced to tiny squares. Each box represented a single week, neatly stacked into rows and columns. The filled-in boxes were stark and shaded, showing the weeks I had already lived. The rest—rows of clean, empty squares—projected the weeks I might have left if I live to eighty-five (and for the record, I plan to blow past that number).

At first, I just stared at it. The shaded boxes felt heavy, like stones laid one after another, a trail of time already spent. And the empty ones? They stretched out before me, a fragile promise. Each week that passes, I'm supposed to fill in another box—another week lived, another week gone forever.

It was sobering. In that moment, time didn't just feel finite; it felt real—something I could see and touch. As Andy Dufresne says in *The Shawshank Redemption*, "Get busy living, or get busy dying."

That calendar now sits on my desk, a silent but persistent stare. It demands that I never play it small. It's not just a reminder of how fleeting time is, it's a call to action.

If I'm going to live, I need to *live* with purpose, clarity, and courage. If I'm going to dream, my dreams need to be big enough to shake me out of comfort and into action. If I'm going to love, I need to love with a fierceness that leaves no doubt about the kind of man I am.

Because those empty boxes won't fill themselves in. The weeks will keep slipping by, whether I act or not. The only question that matters is this: Will I make them count?

By now, I hope you have a sense of just how special the culture we created during our coaching days truly was. We challenged our athletes, both on and off the field, demanding nothing less than their best. But it wasn't just about physical performance, it was about shaping their mindset, their character, and their belief in what was possible.

A significant part of that challenge was encouraging them to think big, act decisively, and embrace a bold vision for their lives. We wanted them to see themselves not just as athletes, but as leaders, dreamers, and doers—people capable of achieving extraordinary things.

To bring that to life, Frankie and I devised an experience that would stretch their imaginations and redefine their sense of self-belief. We called it "Come as You Are."

The premise of Come as You Are was simple. We challenged each player to create a presentation for the team and coaching staff in which they would articulate a bold vision for their future. But this wasn't just a dream session—it was about owning the life they wanted to build.

We set three clear rules:

1. They couldn't limit their vision to simply becoming a professional athlete.
2. Their vision had to be audacious—something that pushed the boundaries of their comfort zone.
3. They had to present their vision as though they were *already living it*, speaking entirely in the present tense.

We pushed them to get specific and think through the smallest details. Where do they live? What does their family life look like? What kind of car do they drive? What house do they own? What business or career have they built? What charities do they start?

If professional sports were part of their vision, that was fine. But it couldn't stop there. This exercise required them to imagine a complete picture of the life they wanted to create—one that extended far beyond the field, into every aspect of who they could become.

When we introduced Come as You Are to the team, we held our breath. We knew we were asking a lot. This exercise required them to do more than just think boldly; it asked them to stand up in front of their peers and declare their dreams—a vulnerable and daunting task for teenagers.

And yet, when the day came for them to present their visions, what unfolded left us completely in awe. These young men poured their hearts into the exercise, stepping into futures that were as bold as they were creative. One by one, they stood before us, turning the room into a place of possibility.

One player arrived dressed as a doctor, a white lab coat buttoned over his chest, a stethoscope draped around his neck. He spoke with confidence, already living the life he envisioned, describing the patients he would treat and the impact he would make.

Another player walked in wearing a sharp suit, presenting himself as the founder of a private equity firm. He spoke of the deals he had closed, the businesses he had built, and the lives he had changed through his work.

Then there was the young man who envisioned himself as the senator of North Carolina. He came prepared, carrying campaign signs emblazoned with his name, his words full of conviction as he described his vision for leadership and service.

Each presentation was a revelation—not just of their dreams, but of who they were and who they were becoming.

It took our breath away.

Some of us sat forward, eyes wide. Others leaned back, arms crossed, stunned into silence. More than once, I caught a coach blinking away tears. The confidence, creativity, and boldness they displayed that day were extraordinary. Each presentation was a powerful reminder of what we already knew: These young men had the potential for greatness. All they needed was permission to believe it for themselves.

What started as an exercise became something far more significant—it became an identity. Come as You Are wasn't just about imagining the future. It was about empowering these athletes to take ownership of their dreams, to step boldly into who they could become, and to see themselves as capable of achieving it.

The Come as You Are event stands out as one of my favorite off-the-field experiences as a member of the Peddie community. It was more than just an evening—it was a testament to the masterclass in leadership that Coach Malleo and Coach Kineavy delivered every single day. Events like this reminded us of their unique ability to elevate everyone around them, pushing us to think and act bigger than we ever thought possible.

Coach Malleo always found a way to draw out every ounce of potential within us. Coach Malleo inspired us through his powerful words and deep relationships, while Coach Kineavy led through his authenticity. Together, they created a culture where it wasn't just about becoming better athletes—it was about becoming better people.

I'll never forget the atmosphere in that room—a group of talented athletes, all discussing their futures with such conviction that it felt like they weren't just dreaming it but living it in that very moment. It was an experience that made us believe anything was possible.

Being part of something like that was nothing short of incredible. It wasn't just leadership, it was leadership at its finest. Coach Malleo and Coach Kineavy didn't just teach us how to be better, they showed us how to believe in ourselves and in each other.

Luke Johnson
OL, Peddie Football (2017–2019)
OL, University of Virginia Football, '24

Over the years, I've collected dozens of photos and videos from those presentations with players in lab coats or three-piece suits, carrying campaign signs, you name it. I keep them on an external hard drive, organized by year like a proud librarian.

Every once in a while, I'll be sitting at my desk and think of a player—maybe one who's away at college, maybe one who just posted about starting a new job. I'll scroll through the archive, find *that* moment, and send it to him. No message. Just the clip. A few minutes later, I'll usually get something back: "Man—I'm getting close," or "Still chasing it, Coach."

But I know what they mean. They remember who they said they wanted to become. And for a moment, that belief gets reignited. That's why I keep the archive. A gentle reminder of the bold vision they once dared to declare and the limitless potential still inside them.

What excites me most is seeing so many of them on the path to, or even achieving, the very goals they shared with our team that day. Some are living those bold visions. Others are fighting to bring them to life. Watching their dreams unfold, step by step, reaffirms a truth I've come to hold close: There is incredible power in clarity, confidence, and a deep commitment to a bold vision.

> There is incredible power in clarity, confidence, and a deep commitment to a bold vision.

Those presentations weren't just words spoken in a room. They were the seeds of something extraordinary—seeds that, with time, effort, and belief, have begun to bloom.

A bold vision gives direction to your effort. It brings clarity when the path ahead is uncertain. It doesn't need to be flashy. It just needs to be true and backed by action. That's the difference between a fantasy and a future.

You don't have to be extraordinary to have a bold vision. But chasing one will make you extraordinary.

Frankie didn't wait for the stars to align. He acted. Boldly. Daily. On purpose. He didn't dwell on what he couldn't do. He leaned into what he could. His vision didn't shrink to fit the world's expectations, rather it challenged the world to rise to his.

Just look at what he's done: coached on a national championship basketball team, delivered TEDx talks that left crowds both laughing and tearing up, written and directed an original stage play, and was named Citizen of the Year. And now? He's helping write a book that will encourage others to live and lead more boldly.

And if you ask him he'll still say, "I'm just getting started."

Let his story be your reminder: Bold vision doesn't start later. It starts now.

So what's your bold vision? What have you been waiting to say, start, build, or become? Picture it. Write it down. Then take the first step. You don't need permission. You just need to begin. Because time's not waiting. And the boxes keep filling in. The calendar has your name on it. Make the days count.

POWERFUL WAYS TO PURSUE A BOLD VISION

CLEARLY DEFINE YOUR VISION

Take time to articulate what a bold vision looks like for you. Be specific: What do you want to achieve? Why does it matter to you? Write it down in vivid detail and imagine it as though it's already a reality. Use visualization techniques to see yourself living your dream. This mental practice strengthens your belief in its possibility.

START BEFORE YOU'RE READY

Don't wait for perfect conditions or until you can summon complete confidence. Take the first step today, even if it's small or imperfect. Bold visions require action, not perfection. Identify one immediate step you can take to move closer to your vision and commit to completing it within twenty-four hours.

BREAK IT DOWN INTO MANAGEABLE STEPS

Break down your bold vision into a series of smaller, actionable milestones. Create a roadmap that outlines what needs to be done and by when. Celebrate progress along the way, no matter how incremental. These small wins will keep you motivated and focused.

CULTIVATE CONSISTENCY

Commit to daily, disciplined actions that align with your vision. Consistency, even in small efforts, compounds over time to create extraordinary results. Establish habits or routines that make progress toward your vision a natural part of your day.

TAKE INSPIRED RISKS

Bold visions require bold actions. Be willing to step into uncertainty and take calculated risks that move you closer to your goal. Trust your instincts and embrace the discomfort of stepping outside your usual limits.

By implementing these steps, you can make your bold vision into reality, inspiring yourself and others along the way.

IN THE WORDS OF THOSE WHO LIVED IT

My time with Peddie Football was one of the most incredible experiences of my life. It wasn't just about winning games, it was about becoming a better man, learning resilience, and being a part of something much bigger than yourself. Coach Malleo's leadership was instrumental in shaping not only my skills as a player but also my character off the field. He pushed us to strive for excellence and led by example. I'll never forget the day we were messing up a drill during practice. Instead of simply walking us through it or screaming at us to get it right like most coaches would have, he actually put on pads, and we hit each other at full speed. It's a legendary story, but he showed us all the intensity and heart he expected from us. Equally impactful was Coach K, who, despite living with cerebral palsy, was a critical part of the team. Coach K's dedication and reliability are truly inspiring. He showed up every day and contributed in ways that reminded us that despite your circumstances you can achieve whatever you put your mind to.

Moments like Come as You Are where we embodied who we wanted to become in the future gave me the chance to reflect on my goals and fueled my ambition to be the best version of myself. It was these little things that made Peddie football feel like more than just a team; it was a family. The intense winter workouts prepared me not just for the season but for life's challenges. They taught me to embrace discomfort and find strength in hard work. Peddie football, Coach Malleo, and Coach Kineavy instilled in me a mindset of perseverance, and I carry those lessons with me every day. I wouldn't be the player or the man I am today without it. It was a special experience made special by the men who led us.

Jack Barnes
LB, Peddie Football (2017–2019)
LB/DE, Bucknell University Football, '24

Courage Is a Muscle, Exercise It!

> The seeds of doubt will always come in, but you don't have
> to let them take root in the garden of your mind.
> —JON GORDON

HEADING INTO OUR FOURTH SEASON, our coaching staff, fueled by Frankie's visionary leadership, had already given us one of our most important truths: Courage isn't something you're born with—it's something you build. He elevated the program to a level no one could've predicted. What began as a scrappy group of hopefuls had become a team of disciplined young men who embodied our mission statement: *To develop young men of character and integrity through the pursuit of excellence on and off the field.*

This wasn't just a motto. It was our DNA. Every coach, every player, lived it.

When we first arrived, our weight room was empty after practice. Players went through the motions, hopeful for wins but unsure of who they were or what they could become. Four years later, it was different. The weight room was full, even when practice ended. Film sessions stretched late into the evening—not because we asked, but because players insisted. Leadership council meetings became sacred ground. Team standards were player-enforced. The culture had shifted.

By now, our roster was still small—never more than twenty-five guys—but pound for pound, we were one of the toughest teams in the state. And people noticed.

Each spring, our campus turned into a mini-NFL Combine. College coaches from across the country roamed the sidelines with clipboards in hand, eyes locked on our drills. I remember the first time an ACC coach stepped onto our practice field—Dabo Swinney from the national champion Clemson Tigers. For us, that was a turning point. Before, we had to send out highlight tapes and hope someone watched. Now, recruiters were showing up unannounced.

Our underdog days weren't behind us, but they had become our origin story.

One of the players who was set to capture everyone's attention that spring was our starting quarterback, Davis Warren. His name carried a certain charisma, and he lived up to it in every way. A California kid with California cool, Davis had sun-kissed blond hair and a magnetic smile that could disarm even the toughest critic. Teachers marveled at his academic brilliance—his grades were the kind that made Ivy League admissions officers weak in the knees. David also had an arm so powerful and precise it left SEC coaches daydreaming about national championships.

No one is truly perfect, but Davis was as close as you could get. That spring was shaping up to be a pivotal moment in his journey. It would mark his junior season, his first as the starting quarterback, and the beginning of his arc from a promising talent to a nationally recognized one. At that point, the accolades hadn't caught up to his potential, but I knew they would. This recruiting period was his launching pad. Once college coaches saw him throw, I was certain his mailbox—and inbox—would overflow with scholarship offers.

That spring, our tiny little school, The Peddie School, became one of the most sought-after stops on the college recruiting tour. Coaches from across the country flocked to our campus, eager to evaluate the talent we had nurtured. To make the most of this golden opportunity, we orchestrated what we called College Showcase Workouts—a finely tuned spectacle designed to put our athletes front and center. It wasn't just a practice; it was a performance.

For any random passerby, the scene might have looked like a whirlwind of chaos. Over fifty college coaches lined the sidelines, each proudly wearing their school's colors, clutching stopwatches, clipboards, and cameras. Their voices mingled with the sounds of drills, the sharp whistle blasts, and the rhythmic thud of cleats pounding against the turf. The field buzzed with possibility. To the untrained eye, it was pandemonium. To us, it was an opportunity.

Every detail of those workouts was choreographed to perfection. Players rotated seamlessly through stations tailored to highlight their strengths. Quarterbacks launched flawless spirals, wide receivers stretched to snag them, and linemen pushed sleds with gritted teeth. It wasn't just a collection of drills—it was a showcase of dreams in motion.

What emerged from those chaotic-looking workouts were moments that changed lives. Coaches left our fields full of excitement, already planning their follow-ups. And for many of our players, those afternoons marked the beginning of new futures—doors opening to opportunities they had only dared to dream of.

From a logistical standpoint, planning and executing these events demanded a near-obsessive level of detail. I knew what was at stake—not just for me, but for the players whose futures could be altered in a single afternoon. That weight wasn't lost on me. I poured myself into the preparations, tweaking schedules, refining drills, and rehearsing every scenario in my mind until the entire showcase felt like a finely tuned machine. It had to be perfect, and

I carried the pressure of that responsibility on my shoulders. But by now, I had it down to a science.

Still, even the most disciplined minds need a break, a moment to breathe before the chaos descends. And so, with the busiest week of the year looming, my wife, Ashley, and I decided to carve out a night for ourselves. It was a chance to reconnect and enjoy a fleeting moment of calm before life's whirlwind swept us back up. We were expecting our first child—a chapter of joy and uncertainty—and I wanted to savor this time with her.

The spring weather in New Jersey was beginning to show its softer side. The chill of winter had faded, replaced by warm breezes that carried the promise of brighter days. Ashley wore a red-and-white polka dot dress that clung delicately to her growing baby bump. She looked radiant, glowing in a way only expectant mothers can.

We slipped into the car, the sunroof open to welcome the golden hour light. As we drove toward one of our favorite dinner spots, the warm air wrapped around us, and for a moment, the world seemed to stand still. We talked about the baby, laughing and wondering what this new life would bring. Then, out of nowhere, she placed her hand on her stomach, her eyes widening. "I felt the baby kick!" she exclaimed.

I quickly placed my hand next to hers, and there it was—a faint, unmistakable movement. A tiny life announcing its presence. We both broke into smiles that could've lit up the entire highway. It felt surreal, like a scene from a movie where everything in life aligns perfectly, if only for a moment.

But perfection doesn't last. Suddenly, the dashboard lit up with an incoming call. "Jeff Warren," it read. Davis's father. Jeff and I had a good rapport and spoke often, so I didn't think much of it. I answered, my voice full of the energy of a man with a beautiful wife, a baby on the way, and a life that felt like it couldn't be better.

"Hey, Jeff!" I greeted him, my tone bright. The voice on the other end wasn't what I expected. It wasn't warm or casual. It was strained, almost shaky. A gut instinct hit me before he said another word. Something was wrong.

"Do you have a minute?" Jeff asked, his voice trembling slightly.

"Of course," I replied, still riding the high of that perfect moment, unaware of the storm about to hit.

Jeff hesitated, and then the words came, each one cutting deeper than the last. "Davis has just been diagnosed with cancer."

The world stopped. The air seemed to disappear from the car, and the joy I had been basking in only moments earlier was replaced with a cold weight pressing on my chest. Memories of my mom's battle with illness came rushing back, raw and relentless. It felt like history was repeating itself in the cruelest way possible.

I instinctively pulled the car over to the side of the road, my hands trembling on the steering wheel. This no longer felt like a movie. The idyllic drive, the laughter, the joy—all of it was shattered in an instant.

Jeff continued, his voice filled with heartbreak. "Davis hadn't been feeling well," he explained. "He thought it was just fatigue, maybe from all the training. But after a weightlifting session where he felt unusually weak, we decided to get some tests done."

The results were tough to stomach: acute myeloid leukemia, or AML, as it's commonly referred to in the medical community. Jeff's voice cracked as he shared the prognosis. The five-year survival rate was 66 percent—a number that simultaneously carried hope and dread. My mind struggled to process the implications, but my heart was already breaking.

Tears began to stream down my face, slow at first, then uncontrollable. I felt Ashley's hand slip into mine, her grip firm and dependable, grounding me as I tried to absorb the unthinkable. Her presence was an anchor in the emotional storm, and for that, I was deeply grateful.

Jeff continued, laying out the details of the treatment plan in their home state of California with a calmness that I knew was a mask for his own anguish. The plan was still forming, but he wanted Davis and me to talk later that evening. He believed Davis needed someone who understood him and could help him navigate this challenge.

As the call ended, I sat there in silence, my hand still in Ashley's. The sun began to set, casting long shadows across the road. It seemed fitting somehow—the light dimming on what had felt like such a bright, hopeful day.

I thought of Frankie and how many times he had reminded us that courage wasn't loud or flashy. It was just showing up, every day, for the fight. Now it was Davis's turn.

That evening, I called Davis. It was one of the hardest conversations I've ever had, but it was also one of the most profound. We cried together, letting the reality of the moment settle between us. And then, somehow, we laughed. Davis's humor and resilience broke through the darkness. Even in the face of this overwhelming challenge, he exuded a quiet confidence that left me in awe.

We talked about his character, his grit, and his toughness—all the traits that had made him the leader he was. By the end of the call, I made him a promise: I'd speak with him as many times a day as he needed. Whether it was for a pep talk, a strategy session, or just someone to vent to, I'd be there.

As we were about to hang up, Davis stopped me. "Coach," he interrupted.

"Yes, Davis?"

"I'm going to beat this," he said with absolute conviction. "And I'll be back on the field for us on October 4th."

I froze for a moment, his words sinking in. October 4th—the date of the fifth game of the season. Davis had already circled it on the calendar in his hospital room.

He had done the math. By now, he knew every detail about acute myeloid leukemia. He knew the timelines for treatment and recovery, and he had matched that with our schedule. Eight months away. For him, it wasn't just a date, it was a goal.

> October 4th—the date of the fifth game of the season. Davis had already circled it on the calendar in his hospital room.

I had learned never to doubt Davis, but at that moment, the farthest thing from my mind was him suiting up for a football game. All I wanted was to see him healthy and to hear his laugh in person again. But Davis had always been different, always aiming for the extraordinary when others would settle for survival.

The next day, I delivered the news to the coaching staff. Faces fell as I spoke, the weight of the situation settling heavily in the room. Davis wasn't just our quarterback; he was our heartbeat, the player who led by example and made everyone around him better.

I told the staff that Davis would need our support more than ever. His fight was our fight.

Frankie, sitting in his usual seat at the head of the table, raised his hand. He motioned for Josh, one of our young assistant coaches, to read from his communication board.

Josh looked at us, then read what Frankie had typed: "Courage is a muscle. We all need to exercise it, or it will atrophy."

The room was silent, hanging on the weight of his words. Frankie wasn't finished. "This is his moment to be courageous," he continued. "He will be fine."

Frankie's calm, matter-of-fact wisdom cut through the grief and worry. He always had a way of reframing the impossible, turning it into something manageable, something meaningful.

His insight reminded me that this was about all of us stepping up, pushing through the fear, and being the kind of team, the kind of family, that Davis had always believed in.

Frankie was right. This was Davis's moment. If anyone could rise to it, it was him.

Through the spring and summer, Davis and I stayed in constant contact. Hardly a day went by when we didn't check in—sometimes to talk football, sometimes to talk about life, and other times just to laugh at a shared joke. It became a lifeline for both of us, a connection that bridged the physical distance and the challenges he faced.

I had strong relationships in the football world, and when those players—top college athletes and NFL stars—heard about Davis's story, they rallied behind him. Videos began pouring in, messages of encouragement from some of the best in the game. These giants of the sport, icons that Davis had probably grown up idolizing, looked directly into the camera, their voices sincere: "We're rooting for you, Davis. You've got this. We're praying for you, and we know you'll be back out there soon."

Each clip was a shot of inspiration, a reminder to Davis that he wasn't fighting alone. Every time I sent him one of those videos, his response was the same: gratitude and focus. He used their words as fuel.

Jeff, ever the proud father, sent videos of Davis from the children's hospital. Those clips were hard to watch yet impossible to look away from. His once sun-kissed blond hair had been reduced to sparse tufts, and his once-strong frame was now frail from the harshness of treatment. The IV lines and portable medical machines were constant reminders of the battle he was waging. Amid all this, Davis refused to let his circumstances define him.

There he was, standing in the hospital's outdoor quad, a football in his hands. The machines trailed behind him, tethering him to the treatment that was saving his life, yet in Davis's mind, they were invisible. What mattered was the ball, the feel of the laces against his fingers, and the motion of his arm as he threw. His passes didn't have their usual zip or precision, but that wasn't the point. Each toss was a declaration, a small yet powerful act of defiance. While the world around him was consumed by cancer treatments and medical protocols, Davis's mind was fixed on one thing: October 4th.

Frankie was consistent in his quiet support for Davis. Every time I shared an update about him—how he was handling treatments, training for football despite them, or keeping an unshakable attitude—Frankie would nod, his expression thoughtful. Then, he would type the same phrase he'd told us from the beginning: "Courage is a muscle. We have to exercise it." Each time he repeated that phrase, it sank a little deeper into my psyche, reshaping the way I thought about bravery.

Frankie loved coaching Davis. He admired his natural leadership and ability to inspire beyond the field. As Davis went through treatment, Frankie challenged us to see courage in action and reflect it in our own lives.

By the time August rolled around, preseason had begun, and our team was preparing for what we hoped would be a historic season. Davis remained in California, undergoing treatments, but we could still feel his presence. He was on everyone's mind. His fight became a rallying point, a reminder of what true resilience looked like.

As preseason concluded and we shifted our focus to the regular season, I received a call from Jeff. His voice was filled with hope and happiness this time, carrying a tone of good news. Davis was officially cancer free. While he wasn't cleared to play football, he could attend practices and games as a spirited observer, reconnecting with his teammates and the program he loved so deeply.

I was standing on the edge of the field the day Davis and his family arrived on campus. When Davis stepped out of the car, my heart sank. He looked so fragile, like a sapling bending in the wind, his body thin and frail from the treatments that had waged war on him. He was pale, and his T-shirt hung loosely from his shoulders.

I wrapped him in a hug. I could feel every bone beneath my hands—no muscle, no strength, just a skeletal frame that seemed to defy the tenacity of the spirit within. For a moment, football didn't matter. All I cared about was that he was back, alive, and progressing well.

But Davis, being Davis, wasn't thinking about survival. He was thinking about football.

He looked me in the eye and said, "I'll be back October 4th."

We all smiled, not because we believed him, but because smiling felt kinder than admitting we didn't. His optimism was so pure, so absolute, that even if we couldn't see the path, we didn't want to dim his light. For Davis, the date wasn't just a possibility, it was a promise.

We started the season strong, winning our first two games with ease. Davis was a constant presence on the sideline, his spirit lifting the team in ways words never could. He paced up and down the white stripe like a coach in cleats, fist-bumping players, clapping hard after every big hit, and huddling with quarterbacks between drives to talk coverages and reads.

He was still rebuilding day by day and rep by rep. We'd crafted a strict strength plan to help him regain his body, and he followed it like gospel. After practice, when most players were in the locker room or grabbing protein shakes, Davis would stay behind on the field. He moved methodically through quarterback drills, shoulder still healing, frame still thin, but focus razor-sharp.

We tracked every throw, because we had to. His reps were capped, his doctors clear: Do not overdo it. And for the first few weeks, he listened. Five throws. Then ten. Then fifteen.

Then one night, I turned around to talk with a parent. When I looked back, there he was—thirty yards deep, launching darts to our backup receiver. Sweat dripping, jaw set, eyes locked in. No hesitation. No pain. Just the familiar flick of the wrist, like the last eight months had never happened.

I jogged over, ready to shut it down. But before I could speak, he looked at me with a grin and said, "Just warming up, Coach."

And that's who Davis was. No limits. No quit. Just a quiet, steady refusal to let anyone else dictate what he could or couldn't do.

Week by week, his body filled out, the frailty fading as definition returned to his shoulders and arms. His throws had more pop. His balance steadied. Each motion got sharper, cleaner. The zip was coming back. The command. The edge. He still hadn't been cleared to play, but it was evident to everyone watching that he was improving faster than anyone had dared to hope.

Our third opponent was a perennial powerhouse Catholic school from Pennsylvania. They had won the 5A state title in three of the last four years and would go on to win another that season. This game was going to test our talent, our discipline, and our resolve.

Davis didn't make the trip.

He and Jeff were at the Children's Hospital of Pennsylvania for a critical appointment—one that would determine if Davis's blood scans and platelet counts were strong enough for him to be cleared.

On the bus ride up, I sat in silence, whispering the same prayer over and over: *Please. Let it be good news.*

Pregame in the locker room was a blur of routine and anticipation. Coaches scribbled last-minute notes. Players adjusted gear and paced in their headphones. Then the door creaked open behind me.

And Davis walked in.

He didn't speak. He didn't have to. He just stood there with that familiar smirk, shoulders slightly back, chin high. His eyes locked on mine, glinting with something I hadn't seen in months—light. The room froze. It was as if time held its breath.

Then it clicked. The smile. The swagger. The unspoken declaration written across his face: I'm cleared. We didn't need confirmation. We just knew.

The next few moments were chaos—the beautiful kind. Coaches shouted. Players exploded from their routines. Helmets slammed into lockers. Guys jumped and grabbed him, overcome with emotion. There were tears, bear hugs, screams of disbelief and joy. For a moment, it felt like the walls of that locker room might crack under the tidal wave of joy and disbelief.

Frankie wheeled over to me through the pandemonium. He raised an eyebrow. I nodded. "He's back."

Frankie typed: "I told you he would be fine."

"You did."

Another line came through, one he had repeated to us like gospel: "Courage is a muscle. And he exercised it." That moment—raw, unscripted, unforgettable—made me feel like the luckiest coach in the world. I didn't need to say much in the pregame speech that night. Their hearts were already full.

We took the field and played like a team possessed—fast, focused, fearless. Every snap, every hit, every throw carried a deeper purpose. We won 38-9. After the game, the opposing coach approached me, shaking his head in awe. "I've never seen a team play so inspired," he said.

I nodded, my voice barely holding steady. "I've never coached one so inspired."

Although Davis had been cleared to play during our third game, the doctors emphasized caution. His white blood cell count would need continuous monitoring, and his game-day status would remain a week-to-week decision.

October 4th—*the* date—was now just two weeks away.

After our victory against the Pennsylvania powerhouse, we had a bye week that allowed Davis extra time to pour into training. Every afternoon after practice, he stayed behind for throwing sessions, working methodically to rebuild his strength. His recovery was accelerating, but there was still uncertainty: Would the numbers align? Would the doctors clear him again when it mattered most?

That Monday—five days before our showdown with The Hill School—Davis met with his medical team for another round of tests. The decision came later that night: He was officially cleared to play on October 4th.

That red circle Davis had drawn on the calendar months ago? It was no longer just a vision. It was happening.

Gameday came, and the electricity was palpable. Davis was ready. He'd fought through months of pain, doubt, and isolation to reach this moment. But even in that celebration, we didn't lose sight of the teammate who had carried the load in his absence.

Matt Sluka—our starting quarterback—had been phenomenal all season. A dual-threat athlete with uncanny poise, Matt was lighting up defenses and leading our offense with maturity beyond his years. He would go on to be named Offensive Player of the Year, then solidify himself as one of the greatest players in the College of Holy Cross football history.

It wouldn't have been fair to simply pull him off the field. But Matt handled Davis's return with humility and grace, the kind of character every coach dreams of. No resentment. No ego. Just a teammate happy to see his brother back where he belonged.

We came out strong, jumping to an early lead and taking control of the game. By midway through the second quarter, I saw the moment I'd been waiting for. The crowd was already on its feet, and our sideline surged with energy as I gave the signal. Davis snapped on his helmet. It was surreal—this was the exact date Davis had told me he'd be back, and against all odds, here he was.

Frankie was beside me as we sent Davis into the game with the play call. The prudent choice would have been a simple handoff or an easy completion, something to ease him in and let him settle. But this wasn't just another moment—it was a celebration of courage and determination. I called a deep pass play.

I could feel Frankie's eyes on me after I made the call. His expression said it all: *Are you sure?*

I turned to him, smiling. "Courage is a muscle," I said with a wink.

Frankie broke into a grin. He threw his arms into the air, shaking with laughter and leaning his head back in pure joy. Even in his silence, everything this moment stood for showed on his face.

As the play unfolded, time seemed to slow. Davis dropped back, his movements smooth and confident, his eyes scanning the field. Then, with a flick of his wrist, he unleashed a perfect spiral that cut through the air like poetry in motion. The ball landed squarely in the hands of our receiver for a thirty-yard gain that felt like a victory far greater than the yards earned.

The crowd roared, our sideline went wild, and I stood there, watching it all unfold with a full heart. It wasn't just a football play—it was a culmination of courage, belief, grit, and the power of refusing to give up. Against all odds, Davis had done it. On the exact date he had promised, he was back. And in that moment, the game felt bigger than football.

Talk about a gut check. Being diagnosed with cancer at seventeen years old was a reality that hit me like nothing else ever could. But in the middle of that storm, Coach Malleo showed me what it meant to have someone in your corner. True to his word, he called every chance he got. It didn't matter how busy he was or what was going on, he was there. He sent me videos from NFL and college quarterbacks who had heard my story, reminding me that I wasn't alone and that there was still so much to fight for.

I'll never forget how he kept reminding me of something Coach Kineavy always said: "Courage is a muscle." It's a phrase that became a lifeline for me. They made me feel strong when I had every reason to feel weak. They believed in me at a time when I was struggling to believe in myself.

I set a date in my mind—the date of The Hill School game. I told myself I'd be out there, and nothing was going to stand in my way. When the day finally came and I stepped onto that field, it felt like more than just a return to football. It was a return to myself. That first pass was a release of everything I'd been carrying for the past year—all the pain, the treatments, the frustration, the tears. Everything I'd bottled up came pouring out in that single moment.

I can't imagine a better group of men and leaders to walk with me through that journey. Coach Malleo, Coach Kineavy, and my teammates didn't just get me back on the field, they reminded me what it meant to live with purpose and courage. That moment, that pass, was more than just football. It was freedom.

Davis Warren
QB, Peddie Football (2018–2019)
QB, University of Michigan Football, '26
2024 National Champion

Courage isn't something you're born with; it's something you develop. Like any muscle, it grows stronger with use. The first step is always the hardest, but each successive act of courage builds resilience, confidence, and the belief that you can overcome whatever challenges arise.

Benjamin Mee, the author of *We Bought a Zoo*, captured this beautifully when he said: "Sometimes all you need is twenty seconds of insane courage. Just literally twenty seconds of embarrassing bravery. And I promise you, something great will come of it."

This idea resonates, because courage doesn't require a lifetime of confidence. It doesn't demand that you have all the answers or see every step of the journey. Often, it's just about finding a moment—a single breath—to leap into the unknown.

For Davis, courage wasn't just an abstract concept; it was the foundation of his fight. When faced with a life-altering diagnosis, he confronted it with a fearlessness I doubt I'll ever witness again. He didn't know how he was going to get better—he just knew he would. Davis had the courage to declare his recovery before the path was clear.

And he was right. Through sheer determination and belief, Davis overcame his cancer and emerged stronger. Today, he enjoys the spoils of his courage. As a member of the University of Michigan football team, Davis won a national championship and became the Wolverines' starting quarterback. His journey is a testament to the power of courage.

Great leaders like Frankie and Davis understand something essential: Courage isn't about having all the answers. It's about choosing action—decisive, imperfect, and full of heart—even when the future is uncertain.

It might look like speaking up in a room full of resistance. Or making the hard call for the greater good. Or admitting, "I don't know, but I'll figure it out."

When leaders act with that kind of courage, they create a culture where boldness is the norm. Teams stop playing it safe. They lean in. They rise.

Courage is contagious, because it doesn't have to be sustained. It just has to start. In one moment—one decision—you can move past fear and create the momentum to change everything that comes next.

Now think about your own life. How many chances have you let pass because fear told you to wait? And how many unforgettable moments happened because—for just a few seconds—you chose to be brave? What moment in your life is waiting for twenty seconds of insane courage? What decision have you delayed? What fear have you been avoiding? What challenge have you tiptoed around?

Courage doesn't require perfection. It just asks you to move one step, however small, in the direction of your conviction.

The world doesn't need leaders with all the answers. It needs leaders willing to act with integrity, vulnerability, and boldness. Because when you choose bravery, you invite others to do the same. And that ripple effect? It changes teams. It changes communities. It changes lives.

So here's your call to action: Take the next step. Make the bold choice. Speak up. Leap. The moment doesn't need to last long. It only needs to begin.

Because sometimes, twenty seconds of courage really can change everything.

Find your twenty seconds. Take your shot. You're more ready than you think.

POWERFUL WAYS TO CULTIVATE COURAGE

DO ONE THING DAILY THAT SCARES YOU

Push yourself out of your comfort zone with small, intentional actions. Whether it's speaking up in a meeting, trying something new, or starting a conversation, these acts build the habit of courage over time.

EMBRACE FAILURE AS A TEACHER

Take on challenges where failure is a possibility, and see mistakes as opportunities to learn. By reframing failure as growth, you build the courage to take risks without fear of the outcome.

LEAN INTO VULNERABILITY

Share your fears, struggles, or dreams with someone you trust. Vulnerability requires bravery and deepens your connections while building resilience against doubt.

MAKE QUICK DECISIONS

Indecision can paralyze. Practice trusting your instincts by making decisions quickly, even without all the answers. Confidence grows when you act in the face of uncertainty.

Each of these actions strengthens your courage muscles over time, helping you face doubt with confidence and resilience in all areas of life.

IN THE WORDS OF THOSE WHO LIVED IT

I had an older brother who played for Coach Malleo at another program before he took the head coaching job at Peddie. The stories he told me about Coach Malleo almost made him seem mythical. But when I arrived to play for him, I quickly realized that this man and his program were anything but fiction. Simply put, Coach Malleo is the ultimate leader.

How many coaches in the world would hire someone with cerebral palsy to be an integral part of their staff? I can only think of one. Coach Kineavy meant everything to our program. We'd be in the middle of some brutal practices, yet it was impossible to complain or feel sorry for ourselves when we looked to the sideline and saw Coach Kineavy giving everything he had for us. He is an inspiration to us all.

During my time with Coach Malleo and Coach Kineavy, I learned what it meant to strain and fight for what you believe in and to have resilience in the face of any circumstance. Those lessons have built the foundation for my career playing in the Big Ten.

I miss my time at Peddie, but I am so grateful for the coaches who shaped me into the man I am today. I'm excited that this book gives the world an opportunity to hear this remarkable story about two remarkable leaders.

Khalil Majeed
RB/DB, Peddie Football (2017–2019)
DB, Michigan State University, '26

LESSON 8

Commitment + Accountability = Trust

> Earn trust, earn trust, earn trust. Then you can worry about the rest.
>
> —SETH GODIN

BEHIND EVERY JERSEY, beneath every set of pads, beats a heart waiting to be seen.

At a boarding school, coaching football means more than just strategy and wins, it means shaping lives. Many of our players lived in dorms hundreds of miles from home. I felt a deep responsibility to be more than a coach—to be a mentor, a guide, sometimes even a surrogate parent.

As our program grew, so did the responsibility. I couldn't give every player the one-on-one time they deserved, but I was determined to find a way to connect with each of them on a deeper level.

One of the things I loved most about Peddie was its open-door culture. Faculty were encouraged to sit in on each other's classes, not as critics, but as learners. I took full advantage of that. I'd often slip into the back of a classroom, legal pad in hand, watching master teachers command attention, spark curiosity, and connect with students in ways that left a lasting mark.

That's where I began to truly see the overlap between great teaching and great coaching. Different subjects, sure, but the same mission: to inspire growth, ignite belief, and pull the very best out of someone.

One afternoon early in Frankie's first season on staff, I slipped quietly into the back of Pete McClellan's history class. Pete didn't need a title to command a room. He was Peddie—a lifer who had grown up on campus, coached varsity soccer, served as a dean—and somehow still carried himself with the humility of a first-year teacher.

His hair had gone gray, but his energy hadn't aged a day. Quick-witted, self-deprecating, and deeply real, Pete had a gift for making students feel like they mattered. You trusted him almost immediately. And by the time he cracked his first joke, you were already laughing along.

That day, as he paced the front of the classroom, weaving stories of Abraham Lincoln into lessons on leadership, I realized something that would stay with me for years: True leaders don't demand attention. They earn trust, and they earn it by showing up.

Pete wasn't lecturing about Lincoln's victories or political strategy. He focused on something quieter and, in many ways, more powerful.

Lincoln made it a habit to visit soldiers on the front lines during the Civil War. He didn't just send orders from the safety of Washington. He rode out to the camps, sat with his men, asked about their lives, their families, their fears. He listened. He encouraged. He *saw* them. And because he showed up, they didn't just follow him. They fought for him, and for the cause he so deeply believed in.

I sat there, pen frozen above my legal pad, a thought echoing louder than anything else in the room: *That's it. That's what we're missing.*

We didn't need louder speeches or harder practices. We needed someone who would show up beside our players. Someone who would sit with them in the trenches of life. Someone they wouldn't just follow, but fight for. And as soon as the thought formed, I knew exactly who it had to be.

Frankie.

By the time the final bell rang, I wasn't just thinking about it—I was sprinting toward it.

That afternoon, Frankie and I sat down and mapped out a new role: director of player development. His mission wasn't about stats or scouting reports. It was about seeing. Listening. Believing. Helping our players realize they were more than the jerseys on their backs or the games on their schedules. And if we did it right, we wouldn't just build a better football team. We'd build better men.

What started as a simple idea quickly grew into something transformative—but not because we labeled it that way. It was transformative because we saw it. We felt it. We lived it.

It didn't take long for the vision to become real.

A few days later, I caught a glimpse of it: Frankie, wheeling across campus with quiet purpose. A stack of questions in his lap. A player waiting on a bench. They'd sit. They'd talk. Sometimes about football. Mostly about life. Frankie didn't coach them. He *saw* them.

Slowly—almost imperceptibly—you could feel the shift. The locker room got quieter before meetings. The laughs got more real. The work got harder. The brotherhood got stronger. Because when someone really sees you—when they care enough to ask, listen, and believe—you rise.

And I watched it all happen. I watched these kids—some who had built seemingly impenetrable walls—start to let someone in. I watched them shift from guarded to grounded.

> Because when someone really sees you—when they care enough to ask, listen, and believe—you rise.

One of the players Frankie connected most deeply with was Aidan McHugh. The same young man I advocated for during the admission process.

Aidan was easy to overlook on paper. He wasn't the biggest guy or the loudest voice in the room. A third-string quarterback on a talented roster, he blended into the background during most practices. But Frankie saw something different in him.

Through their one-on-one meetings, Frankie came to understand Aidan's story—not only the stats, but also the substance. Aidan had come to Peddie on an academic scholarship from the blue-collar heart of the Pocono Mountains. His father had walked out when he was young, and it had been just his mom and him ever since. She worked long hours cleaning houses, and Aidan often joined her after school, scrubbing floors and dusting shelves to help make ends meet.

Despite everything stacked against him, Aidan never complained. He showed up early, stayed late, and gave everything he had, every single day. Football wasn't just a game to him—it was his release, his identity, and his shot at something more.

Frankie, in his quiet way, made sure the rest of us saw it, too. He didn't praise Aidan with loud fanfare or over-the-top speeches. He simply typed a few words after a workout or a tough practice: "Keep your eye on Aidan. He's got something."

Frankie's one-on-one meetings changed our team. But here's what I didn't expect: It changed me. It made me a better coach, but more than that, it made me a better man. I didn't just see kids running routes or lifting weights, I saw young men wrestling with identity, with pain, with possibility. I saw their hearts. And once you see someone like that, you can't unsee it. You coach differently. You speak differently. You lead differently.

That's what Frankie built.

It wasn't about checking a box or holding a meeting. It was about creating a space where truth was welcome, and masks could come off. And in that space, the culture changed—not by force, but by honesty. Brotherhood wasn't just a word on our locker room wall. It was something we lived.

Frankie built a strong rapport with the team, but he never settled. He was constantly scanning for ways to sharpen our culture and raise our standards. For Frankie, accountability wasn't about checking boxes. It was about connection. About growth. That pursuit led to one of the most defining rituals of our program: commitment cards.

Every Sunday, as we looked ahead to the week's challenges, each player filled out an index card with three goals—one academic, one athletic, and one personal. The goals had to be specific, measurable, and bold.

The goals were as diverse as the kids themselves. Some wanted to improve their tackling technique or run a cleaner route. Others aimed to get a B on a chemistry test or call their grandma every Wednesday. One player who had struggled with time management wrote down a simple, concrete goal: study two hours every night. His grades improved. His confidence grew. His posture changed. He started walking into rooms like he belonged.

Each Monday, we gathered as a team to review the previous week. We'd start with film study and performance grades, but then we shifted to something even more meaningful: the commitment cards.

One by one, players would stand and read their goals aloud—the academic, athletic, and personal growth targets they'd set the week before. Then they'd say whether or not they met them.

It wasn't about shame or finger-pointing. This exercise was about honesty and ownership. If a player had fallen short, he explained why. If he succeeded, he shared what helped him get there. Either way, the room listened.

Each player was paired with an accountability partner, someone who had checked in throughout the week, encouraged them, and would speak up if a teammate wasn't giving his best.

It wasn't about judgment—it was about growth. The kind of growth that only comes from looking each other in the eye and saying, "I gave everything I had," or "I fell short, but I'm going to be better."

Frankie believed that when you create a space where people feel safe enough to own their progress, they'll grow. And they did.

In time, Frankie and I introduced the "accountability draft." We designed a set of metrics for things like grades, study hall attendance, workouts, punctuality, and dorm room cleanliness, and each player was measured by these standards. No detail was too small—hydration and sleep habits became just as integral to our culture as strength and skill. Players were then "drafted" into teams based on their adherence to these standards.

The draft process was revealing. Some of our most talented athletes were drafted in later rounds, their teammates ranking them lower for inconsistent accountability.

For many, this wake-up call could have led to bitterness or defensiveness. Instead, it became a rallying point. Players ranked lower worked harder to climb the draft board to prove they were good athletes and good teammates. Meanwhile, those drafted early took pride in their standing and worked tirelessly to uphold the standards that earned them respect.

One talented player notorious for being late was drafted in the later rounds. He was stunned at first but then began going to study hall early to complete his work and help his teammates stay on task.

He started leading workouts, encouraging others to push harder and reminding them to stay hydrated. His conversion was remarkable. In time, he became one of our most reliable leaders, respected by both teammates and coaches.

The accountability draft reflected the values we wanted our players to embody. We all learned that leadership requires reliability, consistency, and the willingness to excel in the small things. The draft empowered our players to view accountability not as a punishment but as a pathway to growth. It also taught us that accountability not only improves individuals but also strengthens the team and builds a united force.

But building this kind of culture took more than rules and rankings. It took trust. And trust starts with authenticity. Authenticity isn't always easy. It requires a willingness to admit that you're human, because people are drawn to what's real, not what's perfect.

As trust grew between our coaching staff and players, the way we coached fundamentally changed. We transitioned from being directive leaders to facilitators. Practices became their own; the players took ownership of the program, running drills, holding each other accountable, and stepping into leadership roles. We stood back, observing and guiding only when necessary.

This shift didn't happen overnight. It was the result of the trust and accountability we had built together through initiatives like Frankie's one-on-one meetings and the accountability draft. These tools created a culture where players felt empowered to take responsibility for their growth and for each other.

That foundation of trust became our greatest asset during the final moments of a championship game against our rival, The Hun School, which also happened to be my alma mater. The rivalry between Hun and Peddie goes back decades. The schools are close and compete on a variety of sports and academic platforms, but the gridiron battles are particularly fierce and always draw large crowds.

Heading into the week, the atmosphere was electric. This was the game we had circled in red on the calendar from the start. A rivalry that ran deep. Coaches, players, fans—everyone felt the significance of it. But one name was noticeably missing from the roster.

Davis wouldn't be available.

He was still recovering from a recent dip in his white blood cell count and hadn't been cleared to suit up. As hard as he'd worked, and as much as we all wanted that movie-script moment, it wasn't going to happen—at least not for this game.

He'd be on the sidelines, fitted in street clothes and a headset, doing everything he could to support the team. But we knew—we *all* knew—the next man up would have to rise.

Like most Hun-Peddie games, this was a hard-fought battle. Late in the fourth quarter, the score had tipped back and forth, neither team willing to give an inch. It was a contest of wills as much as skill. The environment was electric, the tension of a game that could be decided by a single play.

We were down 28–32, with time running out and The Hun School holding the ball. They faced a critical fourth-and-one, and we called a time-out to strategize. The players jogged to the sideline, their faces streaked with sweat and determination, their breaths coming in short, sharp gasps.

The coaches huddled quickly, throwing out ideas, weighing risks, and preparing to deliver instructions. As I turned to address the team, I felt a familiar presence as Frankie rolled up beside me. He typed a single word: "Trust."

I stared at his board. The simplicity of it cut through the noise. I held up a hand for quiet and locked eyes with my team. "Trust yourselves," I said. "No matter what formation they come out in, trust yourselves and make the right play. We trust you."

The paralyzing grip of our circumstances loosened. Smiles crept across their faces. The tension evaporated, replaced with confidence. They had everything they needed to succeed.

The team jogged back onto the field. The Hun offense lined up, and the crowd erupted in a deafening roar.

One of our players recognized the play immediately. He left his assigned man and cut through the line like a missile. He met the ball carrier in the backfield with a resounding hit, driving him backward. Our sideline exploded.

Peddie ball.

We were still down 28–32 and the clock was ticking, but our offense was driving downfield, inching closer to the goal line and the victory, when disaster struck. Matt Sluka, our starting quarterback, the star of our team and the heartbeat of our offense, went down with an injury on The Hun School's eighteen-yard line.

He limped off the field, his face twisted in pain. Davis, in street clothes, met him at the sideline and threw me an apologetic look. With the championship on the line, our top two quarterbacks stood helpless on the sideline.

I called a time-out, and the coaches and players gathered together. Suggestions flew around.

"Put in one of our best athletes," one coach offered.

"Run the ball. Play it safe," another urged.

The pressure mounted. Then, out of the corner of my eye, I saw Frankie wheeling toward me. "Aidan," he typed.

Aidan. Yes, that Aidan. Our third-string quarterback, who looked more like a student manager than a football player. The five-foot-ten string bean swimming in his oversized uniform. The kid who got more playing time filling in on the JV squad than he did with the varsity. I glanced across the field to the opposite sideline. The Hun School players and coaches smirked, their confidence swelling.

"Aidan?" I repeated back to Frankie, almost in disbelief.

Frankie nodded. His expression was calm. It was like he knew something the rest of us hadn't yet realized.

It was bold. It was unconventional. It was risky. But as I looked at Frankie, I knew he was right.

I called Aidan's name, and he stepped forward, standing directly in front of me. When I looked into his eyes, my doubts disappeared. There was no hesitation, no fear—just a quiet confidence that seemed to fill the moment.

"We trust you," I told him. "You've got this."

He smiled, gave me a quick wink, and then turned to Frankie, offering a fist bump with an assurance that spoke volumes. The moment felt electric, as if we were standing on the edge of something extraordinary.

As Aidan jogged onto the field, I couldn't help but notice how small he looked, his uniform hanging loosely off his slender frame. Noise from The Hun School stands, which were built into a hillside, engulfed the field. The opposing sideline hummed with confident energy as the players jumped up and down, sensing their impending victory.

This play would decide the game.

Aidan stood in the shotgun, his voice carrying over the din as he barked out his cadence. It wasn't the booming command of our usual quarterback—it was quieter, less imposing—but it carried a steadiness that reflected his determination.

The snap came in low, skimming the ground, but Aidan deftly scooped it up off his shoe tops without hesitation. He took a quick drop, bounced into rhythm, and let the ball fly.

I couldn't bring myself to watch the pass. My eyes stayed locked on Aidan as he released the ball and immediately began jumping, craning his neck to see over the line. His face was alight with anticipation, his arms extending outward as if, by sheer force of will, he could guide the ball to its target.

Then, like a miracle unfolding in slow motion, the ball slipped into the arms of our diving receiver. The throw was perfect. The official's arms shot into the air.

Touchdown.

A tidal wave of celebration unleashed from our sideline.

Aidan sprinted toward the end zone, his arms windmilling as he ran, his teammates chasing behind him in a wave of elation. Aidan wasn't the fastest player, but at that instant no one could catch him.

In the stands, Aidan's mom's face was awash in tears, her hands clasped to her chest as she watched her son seize his moment. She had worked so hard for him to have this opportunity, and now she was witnessing its culmination.

Frankie, as always, sat quietly on the sideline, a knowing smile on his face. He understood what no one else in that stadium could see: the depth of Aidan's story. Most people in the stadium only saw a backup quarterback come through in the clutch. But Frankie? Frankie saw the story. He knew Aidan had earned a scholarship to be here, had outworked everyone just to stay on the roster, and never once asked for recognition. Frankie knew because he had listened. He had sat with Aidan, one-on-one, week after week. And in those quiet conversations, he had seen what no stat sheet or highlight reel ever could.

Heart. Grit. Worth.

I've coached a lot of players over the years, but I can count on one hand those with the heart, soul, and work ethic of Aidan. He was likable, smart, and a natural leader on a campus brimming with exceptional leaders. I loved coaching him.

Aidan was the perfect person for that moment. And it took *The ChairLeader* to help me see it.

It was our season on the line, but somehow, it was one of the most relaxed moments I can remember. That was Coach Malleo's gift—he had this incredible ability to make every single player feel like they were an NFL All-Pro. His confidence radiated through the entire team. It wasn't just about believing in himself; it was about making us believe in ourselves.

As I stood on the sideline, waiting for the play call, Coach Malleo turned to me with his signature calm intensity. He said, "After you throw this touchdown, make sure you celebrate like your hair's on fire." Imagine being a seventeen-year-old kid, with everything on the line, and your head coach looks you in the eye and tells you—not hopes, not thinks, but knows—you're about to throw a game-winning touchdown. That kind of belief is contagious.

I stepped onto the field with absolute certainty. Before the play, I fist-bumped Coach Kineavy, and in that moment, I knew we were about to win. The play call was perfect. We knew the coverage they'd be in, and our wide receiver ran the route flawlessly. The ball left my hand, and the rest was history.

The celebration that followed was chaos. It's something I'll carry with me for the rest of my life. That moment wasn't just about a touchdown or a win. It was about trust, belief, and the kind of leadership that inspires people to rise to their very best.

Aidan McHugh
QB/Captain, Peddie Football (2017–2020)
University of Southern California, '24
Teach For America

We finished that season undefeated, with a number-one national prep ranking and our second championship in three years. But the true victory wasn't the record, it was the change in all of us. We had built a team that operated with genuine trust and belief in one another.

Thanks to Frankie's quiet wisdom we learned something simple and profound: Trust turns into belief. Belief turns into greatness.

The best leaders I've known understand that trust is the invisible thread that unites people. Leadership isn't about control—it's about empowering others. It's about creating a culture where people feel safe to speak up, safe to struggle, and safe to grow. That safety comes from accountability. When we hold each other to high standards—not out of judgment, but out of care—we don't just elevate performance. We build character. We build connection.

And when we pair that accountability with real commitment—when we actually do what we say we'll do—we create something rare: authenticity. People stop performing. They start showing up. Fully. And that changes everything.

Here's what I know now: Trust is the foundation. Accountability is the structure. Commitment is the fuel. And when all three align, greatness is not just possible—it's inevitable.

So take the first step. Be real. Make meaningful commitments. Honor them. Speak with clarity. Lead with heart.

Because when you live with trust, accountability, and commitment, you don't just shape teams. You shape people. You shape culture. You shape the kind of legacy that lasts.

POWERFUL WAYS TO BUILD AND INSPIRE TRUST

BE CONSISTENT

Trust is built on reliability. Follow through on your promises, align your actions with your words, and maintain consistent behavior. People trust those they can count on.

SHOW TRANSPARENCY

Be honest and open about your thoughts, decisions, and actions. Transparency eliminates doubt and fosters confidence in your integrity.

TAKE ACCOUNTABILITY

Own your mistakes and take responsibility for your actions. Acknowledging when you fall short demonstrates humility and builds confidence in your reliability.

LEAD BY EXAMPLE

Model the behaviors you expect from others. Demonstrate honesty, respect, and integrity in your own actions to inspire trust in your team, family, or community.

By consistently applying these principles, you can build and strengthen trust in all areas of your life, creating deeper connections, stronger relationships, and more effective teams. Trust is a foundation that, once earned, can support lasting success and mutual respect.

IN THE WORDS OF THOSE WHO LIVED IT

Coach Kineavy and Coach Malleo were more than coaches—they were forces of nature who completely redefined what it meant to lead and inspire. Coach Malleo demanded more from us than we thought we could give, pushing us past our limits and showing us that greatness lies just beyond the edge of our comfort zones. His belief in our potential was empowering.

But Coach Kineavy was the heart of our team. Watching him on the sideline, pouring every ounce of himself into the program, was nothing short of humbling. Here was a man facing challenges most of us can't even imagine, yet every single day, he showed up and gave more than 100 percent. He didn't just inspire us, he made excuses impossible. How could we ever complain or give less than our best when Coach Kineavy was out there proving, with every action, that limitations are nothing compared to determination?

Together, they taught me lessons I'll carry forever: how to fight for what you believe in, how to be accountable to yourself and your team, and how to lead with resilience and heart. The impact they had on me at Peddie didn't just shape the player I became—it shaped the man I am today. I'll always be grateful for their leadership, their belief in me, and the example they set for what it means to live with purpose.

Tyler Tedeschi
LB/Captain, Peddie Football (2015–2017)
The College of William & Mary Football, '20

Live and Lead Through Love

> You can love people without leading them, but you
> cannot lead people without loving them.
>
> —TY BENNETT

WHAT DOES IT MEAN TO LIVE A FANTASTIC LIFE? Is it defined by success, wealth, recognition, or happiness? These pursuits may bring moments of fulfillment, but on their own, they are fleeting. Beneath it all, the secret to a truly meaningful, impactful life can be distilled into one simple word: love.

When love becomes the foundation of your life—guiding your decisions, actions, and relationships—you create connections that endure. Living a life rooted in love doesn't mean chasing perfection or avoiding hardship. It means choosing to show up, again and again, with compassion, kindness, and intention. It's about how you treat others, how you respond to adversity, and how you leave people feeling long after you're gone. And yet, in a world so often defined by achievement and status, it's easy to lose sight of what truly matters. So how do we shift the lens? How do we begin to live from a place of love?

Moments after Peddie knocked off our longtime rival, Blair Academy, to capture our first championship, the field erupted into chaos—the best kind of chaos. Players and students flooded midfield, a sea of joy and uncontainable energy. They jumped, danced, and shouted, their voices blending into one deafening roar of celebration. Above it all, the announcer, a jovial man and one of my favorite people on campus, bellowed over the loudspeakers with pure exhilaration: "Peddie wins! Peddie wins!"

It was the culmination of everything we had worked to build. Watching that success ripple out, shared with the entire school community, was one of the most gratifying moments of my life.

Everyone had a role to play in that victory. The teachers who committed themselves to serving students and staying late to offer extra help. The administrative staff who handled our travel logistics so we could focus on the game. The dining hall team who kept us well-fed and fueled. The athletic trainers who worked tirelessly to ensure our health and safety. The athletic director who felt every win and every loss as deeply as I did. Our strength coach who pushed our players past their limits in the weight room, building not just their physical endurance but their mental toughness as well—preparing them for moments like this. And, of course, the students whose support for one another became the backbone of our community.

This championship was not the result of one person's effort; it was a shared triumph, built on the collective love, effort, and commitment of so many.

Yet, in the middle of the chaos—amid the jumping bodies, shouts of victory, and pats on the back—I spotted Frankie. There he was, weaving through the crowd in his chair, his face lit up by a smile. He wasn't just there; he was alive, basking in the victory he had poured so much of himself into.

Somewhere in the madness, bottles of sparkling cider appeared, snuck onto the field by some overly-excited parents. A cork popped, followed by another, and soon streams of liquid gold shot into the night sky. Laughter and cheers rang out as players doused each other, sparkling cider misting over teammates, students, and anyone lucky enough to be within reach.

But they saved the best for last.

In a display of ultimate admiration and respect, the entire team circled Coach Kineavy—our rock, our leader. Without warning, they unleashed the cider, soaking him from head to toe. He sat there, drenched, grinning ear to ear, his arms raised in surrender to the joy of it all. It was pure, unfiltered, and uncontainable; a celebration of the man as much as the moment.

I stepped back, taking it all in, overwhelmed by the beauty of what I was witnessing. The noise, the chaos, the laughter. It was as if the very air vibrated with life. And there, in the center of it all, was Frankie.

He was drenched, his shirt plastered to his chest, droplets of cider still clinging to his hair and chair. But none of that mattered. He wriggled with excitement, his body alive with the energy of the day, his laughter rising above the noise, rich and unrestrained.

His smile—so infectious, so radiant—rippled through the crowd like a wave, as if everyone there could feel what he felt: that he belonged. Not as an observer, not as a guest, but as the very heart of it all.

It was Frankie's moment as much as it was ours, a reminder of how far we'd come—and how much joy lives in the journey when you have the courage to show up and embrace it.

As the scene unfolded around us, I made my way over to Frankie, a towel in hand, to gently wipe the cider from his face. He looked up at me, his eyes brimming with pride and joy.

Slowly, with deliberate care, he began to type: "L-O-V-E Y-O-U."

Tears welled in my eyes. I leaned in close. "I LOVE YOU, TOO."

But those words weren't just mine. They carried with them the unspoken sentiment of an entire coaching staff and team. Words that reflected the bond we all felt, the respect we all shared, and the love we all held for Frankie.

That moment has stayed close to my heart since.

As I stood there, surrounded by the echoes of celebration—the cheers, the laughter, the spoils of victory—my mind drifted back to the day I met Frankie. I remembered our first interview, our first conversation. Even then, he had challenged me, not with words, but with his presence, forcing me to confront my own struggles and blind spots. Frankie didn't just make me a better coach—he made me a better person.

And now, here we were, celebrating something we had built together. This wasn't just a championship. It was the culmination of trust, effort, and belief; a shared journey that had impacted us all.

Before long, love became second nature in our program. Whether we were breaking out of a huddle, finishing a conversation, or wrapping up a grueling practice, every coach and player made it a point to tell Frankie they loved him—and he always returned it, with sincerity and grace.

In our team, appearances and differences faded into the background. On scorching days, players would pour water into Frankie's mouth or gently place a towel on his head to cool him down. And after victories, there was no distinction, no hesitation. They showered him in cider, cheered for him just as loudly, and made sure he was a part of every moment of celebration.

To them, Frankie wasn't defined by his challenges; he was one of the guys—equally valued, equally loved.

Frankie's love for the team was real, and it impacted us. He taught us to look beyond the surface, to see our shared humanity. He reminded us that love wasn't just a word or a feeling. It was a bridge that connected us, a force that turned teammates into family. And those connections, forged in sincerity and care, were far more important than any scoreboard.

When I first hired Frankie, I'll admit I had my doubts. I wondered how the players would respond. Would they feel uncomfortable? Would they see him as an outsider? Watching them not only embrace him but openly tell him they loved him—without hesitation, without pretense—exceeded anything I could have hoped for.

Looking back, I see just how rare and special that time was. Love wasn't just something we expressed. It was the culture we built, the language we spoke, and the bond that united us. It was the thread woven through every practice, every game, and every celebration.

And at the center of it was Frankie—our anchor, our reminder, our example. A living testament to the truth that love, when given freely and fully, has the power to reshape individuals, teams, and lives.

Shortly after our record-breaking undefeated season, I made the decision to resign as head football coach. Announcing that decision to the team was one of the toughest professional experiences of my life. I stood in the center of Caspersen, the same room where for five years we had created and cultivated a culture that changed lives. It was the room where I introduced Frankie to the team. Where we held the powerful Come as You Are presentations. Where parents and players alike shared in the joy of signing letter of intent paperwork in making the college or university decision that would impact their futures. So much of what defined our program, our family, had happened in this beautiful space.

As I looked around the room, the memories seemed to echo off the walls. The players' faces—some confused, others already tearful—made it almost impossible to speak. Watching them begin to cry broke me, and the tears I had tried to hold back began to fall. Walking away from something I had poured so much of myself into, something we had built from the ground up, felt surreal.

In the back of the room, our athletic director sat quietly, his expression a mix of sadness and understanding. He was just as much a part of the success we had achieved as any of us. Off to the side was Frankie, sitting in his usual spot. I hadn't told him yet—I hadn't had the heart to tell anyone yet. Watching his face as he realized what was happening was almost too much to bear. This was the first time he was hearing it, and I could feel the weight of my words landing not just on him, but on everyone in the room.

It was painful for all of us.

As much as I loved being their coach, I loved being a father and a husband even more. Being a head football coach didn't validate me, but my family did. I had outgrown the job, not in terms of my passion or ability, but in the way life was pulling me toward something new. It was time for me to pass the torch to someone else, someone who could carry on what we had built. Knowing this didn't make the decision any easier, nor did it dull the sting.

Leaving Peddie was one of the hardest things I've ever done, but it was also one of the most necessary. And in that moment, surrounded by the players and staff who had become my second family, I knew I was walking away from something magical.

In our four years together, Frankie and I achieved what some might call the impossible. We won two championships, finished with a number-one national ranking for prep schools, and helped send forty-six players on to play college football—forty of whom received full athletic scholarships (four of the six non-full scholarship athletes went onto Ivy League schools, which do not offer scholarships). Of those, three players went on to win collegiate national championships, two were All-Americans, four were drafted into the NFL, and two play in the Canadian Football League.

For a small school like ours, those numbers are nothing short of staggering, especially when you consider the state of the program when we started. But they aren't just statistics—they're a testament to the collective effort of our athletic staff, our players, and the community we built together. Every one of those accomplishments was born from countless hours of hard work, belief, and a shared purpose that united us all.

Years have passed since I last paced the sideline, the roar of the crowd and the weight of the game consuming my every thought. These days, bedtime stories, action figures, and tea parties have taken the place of whiteboards, whistles, and the never-ending pursuit of perfection on the football field.

But while my role has changed, the lessons I learned during those years still guide me. The values of love, effort, and resilience that once shaped a team now shape my family, my relationships, and the way I move through life.

I remain in close contact with many of the young men I had the privilege of coaching. Some are now playing college football, a few are competing in the NFL, and others are making their mark in the professional world. But regardless of where life has taken them, every call, text, or message ends the same way: "I love you."

Hearing those words fills me with a deep, quiet sense of gratitude and purpose. I know, in the depths of my heart, that I could not have

> These days, bedtime stories, action figures, and tea parties have taken the place of whiteboards, whistles, and the never-ending pursuit of perfection on the football field.

served them with that level of impact if it weren't for Coach Kineavy and the incredible influence he had on me.

My hope is that the culture we built, the environment of trust, effort, and love, will stay with them for years to come. I look forward to the first wedding invitations, to opening Christmas cards with pictures of their growing families, and to hearing stories of the careers they choose and the lives they build.

Because at its core, coaching was never just about football. It was about shaping lives—helping young men become men of purpose, character, and heart. Men who know how to lead, how to serve, and how to love.

Frankie taught me to live and lead through love. Leadership is so often associated with strength, decisiveness, and vision. But at its core, great leadership is about love—love for the people you lead and the mission you serve.

Leading with love doesn't mean being soft or avoiding accountability. It means creating an environment where people feel valued, supported, and inspired to bring their best selves forward. It's about building trust, fostering connection, and empowering others to rise to their full potential.

Love transforms leadership by turning it from a top-down directive into a true partnership. When people feel seen, valued, and cared for, trust grows, collaboration flourishes, and expectations are often exceeded.

At the end of the day, your achievements will be celebrated, but it's your love that will be remembered. The way you lead, the way you treat others, and the way you treat yourself will define your legacy.

Love is the foundation of everything that lasts. It's the force that drives meaningful relationships, fuels personal and collective growth, and inspires those around you. Whether you're coaching a team, raising a family, or building a career, leading with love ensures that your impact will endure far beyond your immediate reach.

Frankie taught me that love isn't just a feeling, it's a deliberate choice. It's in the way you show up, the way you invest in others, and the way you choose connection over division, even when it's hard.

If you want to live a truly fantastic life, start by leading and living through love.

Love guides.

Love uplifts.

Love endures.

And when you lead with love, everything else—success, fulfillment, purpose—falls into place.

HOW TO LIVE AND LEAD THROUGH LOVE

PRIORITIZE PRESENCE OVER PERFECTION
The greatest gift you can offer your family, team, or loved ones is your full presence. People don't need perfection; they need you to show up fully engaged. Put away distractions, actively listen, and immerse yourself in the moment. Your undivided attention fosters deeper connections.

LEAD WITH EMPATHY
Empathy is love in action. It enables you to see the world through another's eyes, creating understanding and compassion. Approach conversations with kindness and curiosity. When conflicts arise, focus on understanding rather than winning.

SERVE OTHERS SELFLESSLY
The essence of love and leadership lies in service. True fulfillment comes from focusing on what you can give rather than what you can gain. Offer help without expecting anything in return. Whether it's supporting a friend or volunteering, selfless service enriches your relationships.

EMBRACE VULNERABILITY
Love and leadership demand courage, and that means showing your true self, even when it feels uncomfortable. Vulnerability paves the way for trust and authentic connections. Share your dreams, fears, and challenges with those close to you. Allow others to see your authentic self.

CHOOSE LOVE OVER FEAR

Fear divides and paralyzes; love unites and builds. Leading and living through love means consistently choosing courage, hope, and kindness over fear and doubt. When faced with uncertainty, ask yourself: "What would love do?" Let that guide your actions.

By incorporating these principles into your life, you can create a legacy of love, connection, and purpose that uplifts everyone around you.

CONCLUSION

Carry the Lessons Forward

THROUGHOUT THIS BOOK, I'VE SHARED MANY STORIES ABOUT FRANKIE—moments that highlight his resilience, wisdom, and the lessons he's taught about personal growth and leadership. But I can't let you turn the final page without sharing one that captures his wit and sense of humor. I hope it brings a smile to your face, just as it did to mine.

We were playing a game against a clearly inferior opponent, and by halftime we were comfortably up by four scores. Despite the lead, I was frustrated—our offensive line was underperforming, and our running game was lackluster. At halftime, we had a serious talk with the offensive line, laying out the improvements we expected to see in the second half.

As the team warmed up after the break, one of our linemen stepped into a soft patch of grass and created a massive sinkhole that went almost to his knee. Thankfully, he wasn't hurt, but it was a concerning moment. I immediately informed the officials, who called over the opposing head coach. Soon, we had a full "brain trust" assembled. Officials, athletic directors, and coaches from both sides all huddled around the hole, debating what to do next.

Amid the commotion, I saw Frankie wheeling over from the sideline. My first thought was, *What is Frankie possibly going to add here?*

The group instinctively parted to make space for him. He gave the hole a quick glance, then wheeled away, motioning for me to follow.

Curious but skeptical, I stepped aside and read his message: "That is the biggest hole the offensive line has created all day."

Frankie was laughing harder than I was, but I couldn't help joining in.

If anyone from the assembled brain trust had glanced over at us, they probably would've wondered why we were doubled over, shaking with laughter in the middle of a serious discussion.

That moment captured one of Frankie's greatest gifts: his ability to find humor even in frustrating or serious situations. It reminded me—and hopefully reminds you—not to take life so seriously that we forget to laugh.

As you close this book, I want you to remember a moment, one that stirred something in you. Maybe it was a story. Maybe it was a sentence. Maybe it was Frankie's voice or presence. Whatever it was, let it take root. This is not just a conclusion. It's a call to action—an invitation to live, love, and lead with greater intention than ever before. The lessons shared here are not just stories; they are a blueprint for a life well-lived, a reminder that our journey is far more than the milestones we chase or the titles we wear. It's about the lives we touch, the strength we discover in adversity, and the courage to live with purpose and conviction.

From the moment you wake each day, know this: You are significant. Not because of what you've accomplished or what you will achieve, but simply because you exist. This truth is universal, something Frankie embraced and reflected in everyone he met. When you recognize your own significance and honor it in others you unlock a power that changes lives.

Living with significance starts with curiosity. It's not just about seeking answers, but about seeing the world through fresh eyes, choosing wonder over assumption, and listening when others might dismiss. Frankie embodied this openness, discovering possibilities where others saw limits, and inviting us to do the same.

True limitations, he showed us, aren't set by circumstances but by mindset. The only real disability is a bad attitude. Through his resilience, we learned that choosing hope, perseverance, and belief outweighs any obstacle we face.

That kind of determination often leads us into uncomfortable places, but that's where growth begins. Growth isn't found in the safety of the known; it's discovered in the moments that stretch us, challenge us, and reveal the truest versions of ourselves.

> When you recognize your own significance and honor it in others you unlock a power that changes lives.

And while this journey can be difficult, it is also something to be celebrated. Life's beauty isn't reserved for the milestones; it's found in the steps, the struggle, and the small moments of grace along the way. Frankie's example reminds us that even the smallest progress is worthy of joy.

Yet life asks for more than endurance—it asks for vision. Having a bold vision means dreaming beyond what feels safe or possible, then stepping forward in faith. Frankie lived this kind of vision, building his future through courage and relentless hope.

At the heart of it all is leadership—not measured by titles or commands, but by authenticity, humility, and service. Frankie didn't need a platform to lead. He led through action, through presence, and through unwavering belief in others.

And above all, his story is a testament to the power of love. Love that heals, bridges divides, and builds something lasting. Love that chooses compassion over fear, connection over control.

As you reflect on these lessons, consider your future. How will you live a life of significance, not just success? What bold vision will you pursue with clarity and courage? How will you choose curiosity and love over fear and judgment? And how will you embrace the discomfort of growth to uncover your full potential?

This book isn't just about Frankie's journey, it's about yours. Life will challenge you; it always does. But it's how you respond that will define your story. Frankie's life reminds us that courage isn't the absence of fear—it's the choice to show up anyway. Love isn't about perfection—it's about intention. Leadership isn't about power—it's about service. And significance isn't earned—it's recognized, in ourselves and in others.

So, as you turn this final page, remember: You are the author of your story. Write it boldly. Write it beautifully. And above all, write it with purpose, love, and the unshakable belief that the best is yet to come. The world doesn't need another bystander—it needs you. Your heart, your vision, your courage.

The next chapter is yours to write. Make it unforgettable.

Three Claps!

EPILOGUE FROM THE CHAIR
BY FRANKIE KINEAVY

MORE THAN HALF A DECADE has passed since Chris and I last stepped foot on the campus of The Peddie School together. In that time, so much has changed. Chris has traded a team of twenty-five for a team of six. He's traded his headset for a briefcase, the smell of fresh-cut grass for suntan lotion and freshly-squeezed orange juice. To no one's surprise, he continues to thrive—not in the way most people expected, but in a way that makes perfect sense to those who know him.

From the moment I met Chris, I knew Hightstown, New Jersey, was merely a layover in his journey. I always imagined his ultimate destination to be places like South Bend, Indiana, Tuscaloosa, Alabama, or Ann Arbor, Michigan. When Chris told me he was calling a life audible and shifting his career to commercial real estate, I should have been more surprised. The man is a born coach. He's given countless young people, many of whom started with no clear path forward, the road map to a successful life. I always thought his destiny was leading a blue-chip football program onto the field every Saturday, guiding them toward a national championship.

But then I turned my thoughts toward my own path, wondering what my inner circle must have envisioned for me on the day of my college graduation. Could anyone have predicted that my best life wouldn't come from writing for a Division I athletic department or being featured in a *New York Times* article? Instead, it was coaching twenty-five kids at a small prep school just off the Garden State Parkway that revealed to me the person I wanted to become.

It was then I realized no one is defined by the life they've led—but by how willing they are to become the person they were meant to be. I also realized it wasn't *what* Chris did that made him so admirable and successful. It was his pursuit of eliminating average from his life that set him apart. Once I understood that, his career decision seemed like a no-brainer.

While Chris has established himself as one of the most successful commercial real estate brokers in Florida, my own journey has taken some unexpected turns. Fate has led me away from the world of journalism. Now, I spend my time writing scripts, being involved in local politics, and, yes, still coaching the greatest team sport the good Lord ever created. My football journey has taken me exactly one exit up the road from Peddie. Today, I'm the assistant offensive coordinator for a head coach who reminds me so much of Chris— selfless, dedicated, and unrelenting in his expectation of excellence from everyone around him.

A few weeks ago, as I was preparing this part of the book, I received a random text from one of our former Peddie players. He wasn't one of the SEC or ACC recruits. He was a scrawny prep school kid who hadn't even played football until high school. To be honest, he drove us coaches a little nutty at times. But for some reason, he and I connected.

The text was simple. He was spending a semester in Australia and wanted to share some of the highlights of his trip and let me know he had met someone special there. On the surface, it might seem like nothing extraordinary, but it meant everything to me. Not many people in my position get texts like that out of the blue.

That moment reminded me of one of Chris's greatest gifts. He never sheltered me. He never asked people to walk on eggshells or worry about saying the "wrong thing" around me. Because of that, I was able to build authentic relationships like the one with this young man. It's those relationships that remind me why the work we did at Peddie, and the lessons we carry forward, matter so much.

This is why I say yes every August, even when it might be easier to move on from coaching. Before my time at The Peddie School, I got into coaching because I loved breaking down film and thriving on competition. But after four years with Coach Malleo, it's the relationships—the bonds built through trust and commitment—that keep me driving forty-five minutes to practice.

Now, it's about so much more than the X's and O's. It's about having lunch with former players, writing letters at the end of the season to managers who became my voice on the field, and knowing that I can be a trusted resource and a steady presence in someone's life. I've come to take tremendous pride in building these connections and serving as a go-to person for the people I coach.

That's the real victory in coaching—the relationships that endure, the trust that grows, and the privilege of helping others succeed both on and off the field.

When people suggest I move on from coaching to free up time for other pursuits, my mind always drifts back to a cold December night at the Mandalay Bay Resort in Las Vegas. I had traveled there with my aide and close friend Tim to attend the baseball winter meetings, hoping to secure a pro scouting job. As I wheeled from one conference room to the next, a woman's voice rang out: "Frankie, is that you?"

It was Marcia DeHond, the mother of Noah DeHond, a former Peddie player and one of our first major recruits. Noah had just finished his freshman season playing for Dabo Swinney at Clemson. Marcia and I caught up later that evening over dinner, and it was there she shared something that took me completely by surprise.

She told me how difficult those two years at Peddie had been for Noah. It was his first time living away from home, and the transition was harder than she ever imagined. Then she thanked me for being a sounding board for her son during one of the most challenging periods of his life.

I was stunned. I thought back to our casual conversations—chatting in the weight room, breaking down film, talking about life. To me, those were just everyday moments. I had no idea they had meant so much to him, giving him the support and stability he needed to navigate those tough years.

Would I have been able to serve in that way for that kid before my time at Peddie? In college, I always saw myself as more of a worker bee than a leader. My disability had shaped me into someone who thrived in the rank and file—a reliable guy who could analyze a problem and craft a solution on paper.

I'm still that guy in many ways, but my time with the Peddie football program gave me something I had never expected before: a platform to discover what Frankie Kineavy, the leader, could look like. It allowed me to step beyond the confines of what I thought was possible and embrace a new version of myself—one who could connect, inspire, and serve in ways I hadn't imagined before.

And in that exploration, I found my voice—not just as a coach, but as a guide, a friend, and as *The ChairLeader.*

PHOTO ALBUM

Photo Credit: William Ward

2019 Varsity Team
A dream realized...
Peddie finishes the season undefeated
as a #1 ranked National Prep School.

Photo Credit: William Ward

Coach Kineavy getting dialed in by evaluating warmups on
game day, accompanied by his scribe and friend, RJ Otto.

Photo Credit: William Ward

Coach Kineavy roaming sidelines during key drive.

Photo Credit: William Ward

Coach Kineavy takes in the action with childhood friend Pat Murray.

Photo Credit: William Ward

Coach Malleo pacing the sidelines, ready for their next matchup.

ACKNOWLEDGMENTS

Any great endeavor takes a village, and this book is no different. So many people have contributed to making this experience not only possible but also extraordinary, and I am deeply grateful to each of you.

First and foremost, to the loves of my life—my wife, Ashley, and children, Maylen, Maverick, Makai, and Marley—you are my everything. You are my heart, joy, strength, and greatest blessings. I thank God every day for choosing you as my tribe and for filling my life with purpose and love. I am endlessly grateful to walk this journey with you.

To my brother Matt and sister Jacqueline, I love you more than words can convey. You've been my constants, my allies, and my greatest supporters. No matter where life takes us, we'll always have each other. I can't wait to see what the next chapter holds for us together.

To Dad, thank you for always challenging me to be better and teaching me to leap boldly, even when the landing was uncertain. Your belief in me has shaped who I am. I love you.

To Rick and Wendy, your constant belief in me and the positivity you bring to our family are gifts I cherish. Thank you for being such an incredible source of encouragement. I love you both deeply.

To Gary and Hope, it's amazing how life can change with a single phone call. Thank you for your support, your belief in this vision, and for embarking on this with me. We have so many more boxes to fill in. I love you.

To all my family and the friends who have become family, your love and guidance are etched into the pages of this story. This book is as much a reflection of your support as it is of my own experience. Thank you!

To Jason Baseden, thank you for believing in me, for your leadership, and for giving me the opportunity to work with Frankie. Your support and vision allowed this program to flourish, even when I felt like I couldn't keep going. You refused to let me land when I was ready to give up, and for that, I am grateful.

To the incredible coaches at Peddie—Mike Tedeschi, Josh Holsopple, Rick Nuel, McNeill Parker, Frank Monello, Pat Loughlin, Austin Frank, Marty Mooney, Frank Delaurentis, Pat Clements, Jim Harris, Jamie Will, Mike Volkmeyer, Bruce Eugene, John Washington, and anyone I may have missed—thank you for validating the potential I saw in Frankie and for helping to bring this story to life. Your collective passion and dedication made this experience unforgettable.

To every player who wore a Peddie uniform during this time—you are the reason we can write this story. Thank you for giving everything to one another and to this program. Coaching you was a privilege I will treasure until the day I die. What we built together was extraordinary because each of you is extraordinary.

To all of my teammates and coaches who have shaped me along the way—CB, DO, DD, PF, RK, RB—your influence has made me the man I am today. Thank you for your wisdom and guidance.

To Frankie Kineavy Sr., Madeline Kineavy, PJ Kineavy, and Annie Kineavy—thank you for embodying the true meaning of love and sacrifice. Your family's strength and devotion inspire me every day. I am in awe of you.

And finally, to Frankie—thank you for believing in me when I struggled to believe in myself. You are the heart and soul of this story, and I am so blessed to be part of your journey. Your courage and spirit have changed my life forever.

ABOUT THE AUTHORS

Chris Malleo is an entrepreneur, author, and speaker devoted to building teams, transforming cultures, and helping people lead with uncommon courage. A former Division I football player at Northwestern University, Chris went on to coach high school football at the Peddie School in New Jersey where he built a nationally ranked program that sent forty-eight

players on to play college football, forty-four on full scholarships, with several reaching the NFL. During his time at the Peddie School, Chris pioneered one of the most remarkable leadership stories in sports by hiring a coach with cerebral palsy.

Today, Chris is an entrepreneur and trusted advisor to executives, families, and organizations across the country. He is the founder of High Impact Man (HIM), his flagship coaching program that equips men to live with integrity, discipline, and purpose. Chris is currently enrolled in Harvard Business School's Authentic Leadership Development program, continuing his mission of teaching leadership, culture, and performance at the highest levels.

Grounded in his Christian faith, Chris lives in Ponte Vedra Beach, Florida, with his wife, Ashley, and their four beautiful children. When he's not speaking or building businesses, you can find him enjoying the outdoors, playing pickleball, or spending time with his family at the beach.

Frankie Kineavy is a proud graduate of Villanova University, where he served as men's basketball manager under Hall of Fame Coach Jay Wright. Born with cerebral palsy, Frankie has spent his life defying expectations and redefining what's possible. He has continually demonstrated that limitations are no match for perseverance and vision.

Frankie's professional journey began with six impactful years as the director of football operations at The Peddie School. Here, his insight, leadership, and ability to connect with players helped cultivate a winning culture. His focus on strategy and teamwork later led him to Robbinsville High School in New Jersey, where he serves as assistant offensive coordinator and "special teams" coach.

Beyond sports, Frankie ventured into creative storytelling by writing and producing a short film, which he hopes to transform into a television series. In 2022, Frankie's dedication to advocacy and community service led him to appear before a US Senate Committee on "Lessons Learned from COVID-19: Highlighting Innovations, Maximizing Inclusive Practices and Overcoming Barriers to Employment for People with Disabilities."

That same year, Frankie was celebrated as Citizen of the Year in Spring Lake, New Jersey—a testament to his contributions to the community and his inspirational life. Today, Frankie speaks to teams, companies, and organizations, sharing his powerful message of courage, connection, and leadership without limits.